The
#ArtOfTwitter

The
#ArtOfTwitter

A Twitter Guide with 114 Powerful Tips
for Artists, Authors, Musicians, Writers,
and Other Creative Professionals

Daniel Parsons
@DKParsonsWriter

The #ArtOfTwitter
A Twitter Guide with 114 Powerful Tips for Artists, Authors, Musicians,
Writers, and Other Creative Professionals

© 2016 Daniel Parsons

First Edition 2016

ISBN: 9781533062048

Category: Business & Economics / E-Commerce / Internet Marketing

CONTENTS

ACKNOWLEDGEMENTS

Although I use the platform every day, it was only recently that I considered writing a book on Twitter. My main reason for doing so was to respond to the curiosity and enthusiasm of many creative professionals I know who have seen my success and wanted to know exactly what I've been doing to get it. Some of them I know personally while others I have met only online. I'd like to thank all of you for your ideas and encouragement.

In particular, I'd like to thank authors Wendy Hobbs and Rob Graham who acted as research guinea pigs, asking all the right questions to ensure that I answered everything authors might want to know.

I also have to thank my editor David Norrington. I'm sure that without his experience and brutally honest advice this book would still be a confusing brain-dump with no logical structure.

And finally, I'd like to thank anyone who takes my advice from this book and uses it to build their own platform as a creative professional. I hope you recommend this book to everyone when you're famous all over the world. Connect with me, @DKParsonsWriter, and let me know what's working for you.

WHAT YOU WILL LEARN FROM THIS BOOK

Authors, artists, musicians, game developers, and other creative professionals are under increasing pressure to promote their work through social media. Even for young creatives (who should be prime candidates for adopting new platforms), trying to keep up-to-date with the endless stream of websites that appear to be "the next big thing" can be overwhelming. It's easy to see why lots of people have trouble deciding how to spend their time effectively online. Social media sites are a black hole for a creative person's time that could otherwise be spent *creating* something. While being a social media ninja can play its part in the road to success, it's impossible to master every site; not because of inability, but because you don't have enough hours in a day.

It's better to focus on one or two sites that you can connect with, and that also benefit your career. That way, you are more likely to stick with them and see long-term results. I chose Twitter because it's currently one of the most influential platforms in the world and home to many of the contacts I wanted to make.

Twitter allows you to showcase your work to around 300 million active users, and that staggering number is growing daily. If used correctly it can change your life, generate a massive fan base of loyal supporters, and help you to build your dream career.

As you can probably tell, I love Twitter. And once you hear my results, and how easy it is to achieve the same success, I think you will as well.

I am a fiction author and, at the time of writing this book, I have over 90,000 followers. My tweets get over half a million impressions every month, and that number is continuously growing. My profile gets visited around 1,200 times per day, and my following grows by up to 200 followers every day. People I don't know in the real world mention me on Twitter more than 800 times every month.

When I contribute to trending subjects on Twitter, my tweets sometimes rival the attention of high profile celebrities and established brands, recently featuring alongside the likes of musician Craig David (who has 298,000 followers), *MTV News* (4.38 million followers), and broadcaster Ryan Seacrest (13.9 million followers). When compared with other authors in my field, my tweets often outperform content from famous writers like Ian Rankin (93,600 followers), James Patterson (90,100 followers), and Margaret Atwood (1.01 million followers).

I regularly get messages from celebrities, other influencers, and people I idolise. I have been tweeted by personal heroes such as John Green, Anthony Horowitz, Derek Landy, Darren Shan, and Ian Rankin, amongst others. These are authors who write in my genres and are highly relevant to me.

If you didn't understand some of the terms I've just used, don't worry – that's what the book will help you to understand.

As I've learned more about Twitter, and how to use it effectively, I've discovered that it opens doors that I'd never anticipated as a newbie user. Instead of me reaching out to influential people, they have started conversations with me.

I'm not telling you all of this to brag. I'm telling you because you need to know the potential of using Twitter, even as someone who is not famous. I'm not famous at all. I can walk down the street in my home town and not be recognised by my neighbours. But on the internet, I have acquired pockets of fame, a diaspora of avid followers from all over the world. As a result, my work has been read in more than 70 countries, which I can attribute entirely to Twitter.

When you accumulate numbers like I have, people start to take notice. They mention you on their blogs. They want you at fundraising events. They listen to you and respect your work. The purpose of this book is to give you a step-by-step guide to achieving similar success.

We'll start with the basics. If you have some experience already of Twitter then the first few chapters may be a recap of what you already know. If you've never used Twitter before, then I will get you up to speed, providing you with all the information you need before you get on to growing a large and interactive following. After we have talked about the basics, we will move on to more advanced tactics to engage with your followers.

Some of the information in this book might be repeated. That's intentional, as I know not everyone will read it from cover to cover. While I recommend doing just that, I know that, for many, *The #ArtOfTwitter* will be a reference book in which chapters will be read at random for quick shots of information. As a result, I've tried to give context to related concepts in various sections. That way, everybody will get all of the information they need to turn the following lessons into immediate action.

While I have approached Twitter myself as a writer, what I'm going to show you are transferrable skills that can be used by writers, artists, musicians, game developers, and other creative professionals. With a bit of creativity you shouldn't have a problem putting my advice into practice, whatever your area of work.

Don't be put off if you don't master everything right away. It's taken me almost four years to get to this stage, but it's also true that I could have achieved the same following faster had I known at the beginning what I know now. Fortunately, you won't have that same problem. Reading this book will equip you with the most up-to-date Twitter knowledge, and some information that Twitter tries to keep secret. I'll give you tips that I wish I had known in my early days, and let you know how to avoid the mistakes I made.

At the end of each chapter is a checklist that breaks down everything that has been discussed. There are 114 checkpoints in total throughout the book. Using them should make it easier for you to digest the information and convert it into actionable steps, offering you a fast-track to the heart of the Twitter universe.

The first users are often the most successful on any new social media site. That's true of Twitter in most cases. The earliest users who opened their accounts in 2006 when Twitter's growth rules were more relaxed may now have hundreds of thousands of followers. However, follower-count alone is not your ultimate goal. In spite of their impressive number of followers, many of these people are not as successful as they could be. The amount of engagement their tweets receive is miniscule by comparison to users who use their accounts in smarter ways. I have seen accounts with over a million followers who don't get even a single interaction when they tweet. That's not what we want to see.

I joined Twitter in August 2012. Even coming to the party so late, I have a Klout score (a measurement of online influence) that rivals many A-list authors and I get a higher level of engagement relative to my number of followers per tweet than many celebrities. We'll talk more about Klout later. For the moment it's useful to know that it's a meaningful measure of your social media presence and influence.

You don't have to be an early adopter to be successful on Twitter. There is still time to join. You aren't out of the game before you even begin.

Before we begin learning how to master Twitter, I have provided a glossary of terms on the next few pages that will help you blast through the jargon surrounding social media. Feel free to dip back into it as you progress through the book. Knowing the definitions of the right words will reveal to you that social media is actually a simple topic hidden behind a wall of confusing words. Good luck! You'll be tweeting like a pro before you know it.

Glossary

This section will explain lots of common terms associated with Twitter. If you've heard any terms yourself that are not on this list, feel free to tweet me (@dkparsonswriter) and I will clear up any confusion. I also list some of the other social media platforms and websites that I reference in the book.

Twitter Terms

Attachments

Attachments include any form of file or document that can be attached to a message. On Twitter you can attach images and videos to a tweet by clicking the buttons in the bottom left-hand corner of the tweet box.

BOT

On Twitter, bots (short for "robots") are software programs used to automate the mass-creation of fake accounts. They are used by spammers all over the internet. Bots are typically used unethically to deliver fake audiences to paying customers pretending to look successful.

BUFFER

A scheduling app, much like Hootsuite, (see below), but not as popular. Buffer enables users to schedule social media posts months in advance, saving time and energy by focusing their social media activities into batch tasks.

CLICKBAIT

An adjective used to describe images, links, or headlines that are misleading or overly sensational purely for the purpose of getting people to click on them and follow a link to a website.

CLICK FARMS

These are sweatshops, often located in developing countries. They have hundreds of workers who manage fake social media accounts, following customers *en masse* who pay for followers to make their social media presence look more impressive.

DETAIL EXPAND

This just means that someone has clicked on your tweet to see extra information like comments and retweets. Having a lot of detail expands can indicate that your tweets are generating a lot of debate or intrigue even if they aren't getting retweets or likes.

DIRECT MESSAGES

Direct messages (often referred to as "DMs") were, like tweets, limited to 140 characters. They have since been expanded to 10,000 characters. DMs are private and can only be seen by the person you're messaging. Using direct messages is a good way to share personal information. To DM, both users need to follow each other.

FAKE FOLLOWER

This is a fraudulent Twitter account that isn't who it pretends to be. Many fake followers are created by bots and managed by click farm workers in developing countries whose sole job is to follow strangers on the internet in exchange for money.

FOLLOWER

Followers are people who click the *Follow* button to see your tweets in their main Twitter feed. There is no limit to the number of people that can follow you. However, you can only follow around 5,000 other users until you have at least 4,545 followers yourself (yes, it really is that specific).

FOLLOWING

The act of following someone means that you have clicked the *Follow* button presented on their personal profile. As a result, their tweets with show up in your main feed on your Home page.

FOLLOWING-TO-FOLLOWER RATIO

Your following-to-follower ratio is the comparison between the number of people you follow and the number of people that follow you. Following more people than follow you will give you a ratio below one, whereas following fewer people than follow you will give you a ratio above one.

HANDLE

Your handle is your Twitter username. It's the means of identifying and reaching you. It begins with the @ symbol and needs to be included in tweets to reach a user's notifications. Don't confuse it with your name. Your name is how you present yourself on your profile page, but lots of people have the same name. Your handle, on the other hand, is unique. For example, my name is Daniel Parsons but my handle is @DKParsonsWriter.

HASHTAG

Hashtags are words or short messages that begin with the # symbol. They contain no spaces and can only include letters and numbers. If a hashtag contains multiple words, the first letter of each word is often capitalised to improve readability. Hashtags group tweets into searchable categories. For example, using #Glastonbury2016 in a tweet will group it with other tweets that feature the same hashtag. By following a hashtag (which is a clickable link in tweets), any user can see its tweets in reverse chronological order to track comments on topics and events.

HASHTAG GAMES

Daniel Parsons
@dkparsonswriter

"Oh, you're a writer. I wish I had a job where I could do nothing all day, too."
#AndThatsWhenTheFightBrokeOut

RETWEETS 101   LIKES 209

Hashtag games are fun competitions in which a hashtag that encourages creative contributions is made popular by users. Examples include #WhenICameBackFromSpace and #AdviceFromMyPet. The way to win is to get more retweets and favourites than any other contributor.

HOME PAGE

Your home page on Twitter can be found by clicking the top, left-hand button labelled *Home*. It will show a live feed of all the tweets of the people you follow.

IMPRESSION

An impression is a unit of measurement used to gauge every time a person actually sees something on their screen. For example, you might have 1,000 followers, but if only 200 are online to see your latest tweet then that tweet gets 200 impressions.

INTERACTIONS (OR ENGAGEMENTS)

Tweet Activity

Daniel Parsons @dkparsonswriter Stop procrastinating and start now. #NewYearsResolutionIn5Words	Impressions	23,081
	Total engagements	479
	Likes	156
Promote your Tweet Your Tweet has 479 total engagements so far. Get more engagements on this Tweet!	Detail expands	124
	Retweets	117
	Profile clicks	61
Get started	Hashtag clicks	16
	Replies	6
	Follows	1

Twitter counts impressions, profile clicks, and detail expands, as an interaction. The most useful interactions to measure are retweets, likes, replies, and link clicks.

LINK CLICK

A link click is recorded every time someone clicks on a link you provide in a tweet. This can be a link that takes a person away from Twitter to another website. It can also mean that a link has been clicked in order to view an image you have attached to a tweet. This latter example only applies to link clicks from Twitter users on mobile devices where Twitter is presented differently.

LISTS

Lists are collections of Twitter users that have been grouped together by a user. Lists can be collated by any criteria a user wants to use, but are used mainly for organisational purposes. You can create lists and be included in ones made by other people. Care should always be taken when naming lists as users will be informed when they have been included in one.

MEME

The Vet: An Unexpected Journey #DogBooks

Memes are images that include bold text, created with the intention of being funny or satirical. They are often used on social media to offer a commentary on current events. Memes can make your tweets more eye-catching so that they gain more attention.

PINNED TWEET

A pinned tweet is one that you fix to the top of your profile feed, ahead of all other tweets. It can be used as an extension of your biography as it will be the first thing people see when looking at your tweets.

PROFILE

Your profile is your main page on Twitter. It's where you display all of the information you want the world to see. Think of your profile as a way of introducing yourself to strangers. A profile should include:

- A profile image.
- A background image.
- A short biography.
- A feed of all your tweets with the most recent at the top.

PROFILE CLICK

When your tweet receives a profile click, it means that someone has clicked through that tweet to your profile to check out the rest of your tweets.

PROFILE PICTURE

Your profile picture can be an image of you or your company. 400 pixels square is recommended. High resolution images will typically be rejected but that doesn't matter as your profile image will typically be viewed only at thumbnail size. For more info, see "Profile Picture" in the chapter named *Your Twitter Profile*.

REPLY

Replies are just comments that reply to a specific tweet. They are separated from original tweets as they start with a Twitter user's handle. They often get limited exposure when compared to original tweets as they don't interest people who are not involved in the conversation.

RETWEET

If you retweet something, you're actively promoting someone else's tweet to your followers. If you follow someone with 200 followers, their tweets can be seen by 200 people, one being you. If you then retweet their tweets, and you have 500 followers, your followers can also see that original tweet. So the tweet would theoretically reach 700 people. Of course, there could be some overlap. The more retweets you get, the more people you reach.

SPAM

Spam is any message you receive that is automated or salesy in nature. Spam is often intrusive, or else part of some sort of scam.

TRENDING

When a word or hashtag is included in enough tweets to be listed in the top ten most used phrases of a user's Home page feed, it's said to be trending. Typically, things that are trending for one user also trend for others as more people get involved. Trending subjects gain massive levels of exposure. Anyone or anything can trend on Twitter as long as it captures the attention of enough users. Trending and "going viral" mean the same thing.

TROLL

A troll is a person who intentionally tries to offend others or start an argument on the internet. It's unpleasant, and trolling someone can also lead to legal action under certain circumstances.

TWEETS / TWEETING

Tweeting is simply the act of writing a message and posting it for everyone to see. Likewise, tweets are the short messages you send out and receive from other people. They are limited to 140 characters, excluding a person's Twitter handle, links, and images, and are open to be viewed by any other user unless you've protected your tweets (not recommended).

TWITTER FEED

When you follow another user you can see their tweets on your Home page along with all the tweets of everyone you follow. This timeline of tweets is called your main feed and is the best place to get live updates from people you follow. Everyone also has their own personal feed that shows only their own tweets and anything they retweet on their profile page.

UNFOLLOW

In order to unfollow someone, you first have to follow them. When you unfollow a person, you stop seeing their tweets in your main feed unless someone else that you follow retweets a tweet written by the person you unfollowed.

VERIFIED ACCOUNTS

J.K. Rowling ✓
@jk_rowling

Verified accounts are those that have been authenticated by Twitter. They can be identified by the blue and white verification badge that features next to the names of celebrities, influencers, and large corporations.

WEBSITES

Several sites are mentioned in this book, here are some brief details for each of them.

FACEBOOK

Currently the world's largest social media platform. Founded in 2004, Facebook has become a juggernaut in online advertising and social interaction.
www.facebook.com

GOOGLE+

Google+ is Google's social media platform. It is integrated into many websites, most notably YouTube. In order to write a

comment under a YouTube video, you have to have a Google+
account.
www.plus.google.com

HOOTSUITE

A scheduling app that is compatible with both Twitter and
Facebook. Hootsuite enables users to schedule posts on
several social media platforms in one place, and for months in
advance.
www.hootsuite.com

INSTAGRAM

A picture-sharing social media platform owned by Facebook. Its
focus is on images rather than words and this has made it
popular with models, photographers, and people who promote
visual brands.
www.instagram.com

KICKSTARTER

A crowdfunding website in which people set up advertising
campaigns to get creative projects funded by lots of people via
the internet. Each campaign requires a deadline and monetary
goal. All goals must be met before the deadline in order for the
fund to be rewarded to the organiser.
www.kickstarter.com

KLOUT

Klout is a website that can be used to measure a person's
online influence based on the number of followers and
interactions they get on several social media platforms. Klout
scores are displayed as a single number between one and 100,

with each number being harder to achieve than the one before it. The average score is 40.

www.klout.com

LINKEDIN

LinkedIn is a social media platform designed specifically to help business people network. Instead of getting "followers" like on Twitter, people on LinkedIn gain "connections" in order to improve their CV.

www.linkedin.com

MANAGEFLITTER / MANAGEFLITTER PRO

An app that organises the people any Twitter user follows into categories so that they can be more easily managed. The paid option, ManageFlitter Pro, has added capabilities, giving the user the ability to search out new accounts to follow by using a system based on keywords.

www.manageflitter.com

PERISCOPE

A video-streaming app that allows users to record and stream videos on their mobile devices. Each video is only available to the public for a limited amount of time after it is posted. Periscope was designed to be compatible with Twitter but is essentially a separate platform, more like YouTube.

www.periscope.tv

THUNDERCLAP

Thunderclap is an app that can be used to crowd-schedule tweets. This app is useful when running advertising campaigns.

It enables an event organiser to get people to tweet a pre-selected message at the same time. Thunderclap requires a goal and a deadline to run a campaign. This usually consists of a few months and a few hundred participants.

www.thunderclap.it

TUMBLR

Tumblr is a social media platform based around blogging. Its primary demographic is known to be teenage girls.

www.tumblr .com

TWITTER

Twitter is a social media platform with over 300 million active users. Its users can broadcast short messages called *tweets* that are limited to 140 characters. Twitter is about being social and partaking in its social commentary of current events.

www.twitter.com

VINE

A relatively new social media platform in which people post six-second videos, Vine is famously known as YouTube for people with short attention spans. Despite early criticisms, it appears Vine is more than just a passing fad, and has provided careers for a crowd of new-media stars.

www.vine.co

WATTPAD

A story-sharing website where writers can publish their work for anyone to read it for free. Although free, Wattpad has given many writers massive amounts of exposure, leading to lucrative publishing deals and promotional opportunities.

Chapter reads on Wattpad are displayed similarly to YouTube's video views.

www.wattpad.com

YOUTUBE

YouTube was once considered the world's largest video-sharing social network until that mantle was taken up by Facebook. On YouTube, users upload videos for anyone to watch. Content creators are able to make money here by capitalising on YouTube views, advertising, endorsement deals, and merchandise sales.

www.youtube.com

YOUR TWITTER PROFILE

Optimising your Twitter profile from the beginning is the best first step you can take to ensure the long-term success of your account. It provides a powerful foundation that can improve the results of every marketing move you make thereafter. In this section I'll go through each feature of your profile and describe how they can be optimised.

First, however, you need to set up your profile. To do so, simply go to *twitter.com* and create an account. The process is simple, with step-by-step instructions to guide you. Don't worry about optimising your account during this initial process, as the information you enter can be changed later.

WARNING: The only feature of the setup process you do need to consider carefully is your Twitter username. Look at the section entitled *Twitter Handle* further into this chapter. This is vital because your handle or username (same thing) can't easily be changed once it has been created so should be considered carefully before anything else.

As soon as you've finished the initial setup process, we can work on crafting your Twitter profile into its best possible shape.

BRANDING YOUR ACCOUNT

As a creative type, you might see the word "brand" and immediately say, "I'm not a business. I'm a creative person and I won't sell myself like some sleazy salesman!" I completely understand; I also value my creative integrity. No matter what kind of art you create, you probably create your art because you love to do it, not just for money or fame (although, that would be nice!). I'm guessing that you'd probably like more time to create, and to take your hobby or career to the next level. To do that you need to earn enough from your talent to leave your day job, or progress in your career. That's where branding could help you.

By embracing branding, you are recognising that there are two sides to you as a creative professional. There is the normal, everyday 'you', who might be found in the local bar with friends, hurling banter about that time you all got drunk and ran naked through the town. And then there is the professional side of you who publishes your work, gets interviewed, and attends award ceremonies. These may be two very different people, but they are both a part of you. Branding is simply managing how you present yourself to your followers online, and how much of your different sides you actually share.

It's fine to allow your personality and sense of humour to work their way into your professional endeavours – in fact, I encourage it. Your personality can help you to stand out, especially on Twitter. But I would caution you that anything you say on Twitter should match the *professional* you who would be ill-advised to cause unnecessary offence. Just because you can use Twitter at home doesn't mean you have to share *everything* with your followers, just like you probably wouldn't share the "drunkenly running through town naked" story at a boardroom meeting. Unless, of course, that's part of your brand. If you're a stand-up comedian, for example, then using bad language and mocking people may be part of your act and, therefore, part of your brand identity. Posting lots of polite tweets would be out of kilter with that public persona.

That being said, there are still lines you should set yourself and not cross. For example, would you feel comfortable sharing pictures of your children? Where you draw the line on revealing your private self is up to you. Just be aware that there probably should be a boundary.

Twitter is a 24-hour companion, something that's always present. Most people have heard the horror stories of people texting whilst drunk. Those texts are usually sent to just one person. Imagine how damaging it would be to drunk-tweet to an audience of thousands.

Always assess whether you should really be discussing or sharing something on Twitter. If you wouldn't say it at a public event, then the chances are it doesn't fit your brand.

Having said that, you shouldn't completely restrict the zany side of your personality (if you have one). It's true that you don't want to offend people, but you also don't want to sound like a robot that simply replies to fans with vanilla comments. Add some flavour but don't taste unpleasant. You need to identify clearly where your boundaries are when constructing your public persona, and to stick to your own rules for posting.

It's okay to be weird on Twitter. In fact, originality is encouraged. If you're offensive, you will lose most of your audience and attract a certain type of negative user. But if you are actually weird, those of your audience who don't appreciate your quirks will probably gloss over them, or move on to a "safer" set of people to follow. Those who love imagination and strangeness will really engage with you. It will make you memorable and relatable.

Branding helps creative professionals to stand out, especially online. It presents the best, most memorable version of you possible. If done correctly, people will appreciate your artistic vision. Over time they will show that appreciation by supporting your creativity.

TWITTER HANDLE

Daniel Parsons
@dkparsonswriter

In terms of constructing your profile, we'll begin with your handle – your unique identity tag on Twitter. Ideally, it should be your real name, stage name, or pen name, but those are already taken for most people. If that's true for you, at least ensure that your handle is short and memorable. There are two compelling reasons for this:

1) Using your handle is the only way people can contact you. Your followers need to type it correctly to guarantee that you will receive any messages directed your way. My handle is @dkparsonswriter. Obviously, this isn't ideal as it doesn't match the name on my books, which is Daniel Parsons. However, it does include my initials, surname, and my job which should make it

easy to remember for most of my followers. When I opened my account, @DanielParsons, (my first choice), was taken.

2) Your handle needs to be as short as possible. That way, it's easier to remember and less likely to include a typo when people include it in a tweet. Making it easier for your followers to include your handle in tweets will get you mentioned in more places, widening your exposure.

CHANGING A TWITTER HANDLE

Once you've set up your Twitter handle, you can request to change it, but doing so has consequences. If you're verified, you'll lose your verification badge and it could result in a lot of confusion. Had I known at the beginning what I know now, I would have chosen a shorter handle, more consistent with my authorial brand. However, changing it now is too risky for me as it could mean losing followers. That's a lesson learned the hard way!

ACCOUNT NAME

Your name on your Twitter account is the title people see next to your profile picture. It doesn't have to be unique. Most people use this space to include their real name or company name so that their followers know exactly what to call them if their handle doesn't make that obvious.

Daniel Parsons
@dkparsonswriter

For the creative professional, I would suggest either providing your real name, pen name, or stage name – whichever is consistent with your brand. You should avoid labelling yourself as the title of your latest work, or a character, simply because you would have to keep rebranding as you move onto newer projects. Too many times have I seen authors create a Twitter account in the name of their debut novel, instead of after themselves, and then abandon the account and start fresh when they release another book. Using your own name keeps your Twitter identity consistent and allows for better long-term growth.

PROFILE PICTURE

The effectiveness of your profile picture depends entirely on what you are trying to convey. As a creative person, you're probably going to need a picture of yourself. Try not to use a drunken Facebook photo or a holiday snap, as these images make you look unprofessional – that is, unless you're a travel writer or you write books about partying, in which case these images may be perfect for your brand.

In most cases the best approach is to take a head and shoulders picture in which you're dressed in smart-casual clothes and you are looking into the camera. Not only does this make you look professional without looking too formal, but followers engage with your eyes.

As a final note on profile pictures, at least make sure you have one. Accounts with a standard Twitter egg placeholder often put off users and have considerably lower levels of engagement. Even a bad profile picture is better than nothing at all (as long as it's not offensive).

BIOGRAPHY

Daniel Parsons

@dkparsonswriter

UK Author of fantasy adventures
#TheWinterFreakShow & #Blott. Cardiff
Uni graduate, Wattpadder, speaker, &
wannabe explorer. I don't read DMs
often.

Your biography, or "bio," is a short passage that describes you. It's limited to 160 characters and is situated under your image on your profile page.

If you want intelligent, creative people to follow you then you need to show that you are also intelligent and creative. You should write in a good standard of English and include a few interesting details about yourself.

Include words that relate to your field, whether that be "author," "painter," "lecturer," or whatever. These words can be found by search engines, exposing your profile to a wider audience beyond Twitter alone. Implying that you have authority in your subject is also proven to increase your follower growth. For example, users tend to attract more followers if they refer to themselves as an author rather than a writer, or if they state that they are a keynote speaker instead of saying that they "do talks."

In contrast, you should avoid terms that make you look like a spammer, selling whatever it is you create. By all means include the names of things you've created as they can make you recognisable, but don't suggest that people go and buy

24

them immediately. As your bio is likely to be one of the first things your prospective followers will see, you'll want to give them a good first impression, showing that you're a creative, interesting person, not just a selling machine.

Some people also include something light, possibly a joke, to clinch the deal when someone is deciding whether or not they want to follow them. Remember, people like to be entertained. If your bio is entertaining, then it's a good indication that your tweets will be as well. You don't have to do this, but it can be very effective if it matches your personality.

IMAGES

Images used for your profile picture should be at least 400 x 400 pixels, whereas images for your background (the long image across the top of your profile) should be around 500 pixels high x 1500 pixels wide. If you're planning to use images in your tweets, they need to be at least 700 pixels wide. Narrower images result in an image that looks unsightly, not stretching across the whole of your tweet's allocated space.

LINKS

In your Twitter profile you're given the option to include one link. This should act as an extension of your bio, driving visitors towards more information about you and your work. If you have a website, blog, YouTube channel, or Facebook page, the link section below your bio is the best place to present it. Choose your best link and include it there.

I would recommend leaving your bio itself link-free. That way, you create a good first impression when introducing yourself without seeming like a pushy salesperson. Remember,

Twitter is about being social. Be an approachable person first, and allow people to become interested in you. They will know where to look for your work if you provide a link in the relevant section.

PINNED TWEETS

A pinned tweet is one that can be fixed to the top of your profile feed, ahead of more recent tweets. It can be used as an extension of your bio as it will be the first thing people see when looking at your tweets. The best ways for creative professionals to use this feature are either to use it to promote your work – possibly by asking visitors to sign up to your mailing list – or to pin something profound or funny here. Both will generate a constant trickle of interactions from users whenever they discover your Twitter profile for the first time.

The former will generate mailing list sign-ups, whereas the latter will provide a constant buzz of interactions, extending your reach on Twitter. If you're aim is this second goal then consider this: having a pinned tweet that isn't relatable will not generate this continuous buzz. If people don't relate with it, they won't share it with their followers, no matter how clever or funny you think it is.

I change my pinned tweet every few months to refresh my page, usually by choosing a more recent tweet that has had a large amount of retweets. As a guideline, I would encourage this practice, analysing which tweets have done well in the past and pinning them as they will probably inspire more interactions in the long run.

VERIFIED ACCOUNTS

Verified accounts came about as a solution to distinguish

true celebrity accounts from imposters and parody accounts. Twitter will systematically verify accounts from their headquarters.

If you feel that you need to be verified then you must be patient as Twitter verifies most eligible accounts automatically and doesn't have an official application process.

As I write this book, there are just over 170,000 verified Twitter accounts in existence. Verified accounts have a white tick in a blue badge next to wherever their name is presented on Twitter. People and businesses often get verified to prove that they are exactly who they say they are. It's a way of protecting celebrities, politicians, and companies from being slanderously impersonated.

Getting your account verified indicates that you're a prominent figure in your field. As an author, artist, or musician, this can grab people's attention, offering a level of credibility to your work that you could never convey yourself to a stranger. It's evidence that you're a social powerhouse and will make people want to know you the moment they spot your verified badge, even if they've never heard of you.

Twitter has an entire department dedicated to verifying accounts. Occasionally, prominent figures get verified automatically without them ever having to do anything. Most people think that this is how it works for all accounts. However, the truth is that Twitter doesn't always step in like a god and verify popular figures as soon as they start gaining attention. Often – and most people don't realise this – account owners actively pursue verification before they get verified. There is no official, public way of doing so. Indeed, the process for applying to get your Twitter account verified is more secretive than Area 51. If it were easy to find, everyone would apply. But it is possible.

The way to apply is very frustrating for the majority of people as it involves someone saying, "I know a guy who knows a guy who can hit me up." The alternative is working for a company where the boss "knows a guys at Twitter." This is mainly annoying because, like most of us, I don't know a guy at Twitter. Getting what you want in life, whether it's a job, an internship, or a place in a competition, can often be helped by having a contact on the inside – and it's the same with Twitter, to a degree. To my knowledge, there is no other way of achieving your verification badge.

If you don't know a guy or work for a company that can request the application form for you then you will probably just have to be patient and work hard at whatever it is you do. Catching the attention of Twitter's employees can take time if you have to do it naturally, but the hard work will be totally worth it.

If you're successful and you become verified then this will definitely make your account stand out, leading to a significant boost in interest. The platform this extra attention offers you will help you take your creative brand to the next level.

WHAT NOT TO PUT IN YOUR PROFILE

If you want to know what not to put in your profile, simply look at "Who Not to Follow" in the chapter entitled "Following and Followers." There you will find lots of examples of bad practices when setting up a Twitter profile, as well as things that immediately make people reconsider hitting the Follow button.

PROFILE SETUP CHECKLIST

In summary, to create an effective profile on Twitter, you should:

- o Brand your account.
- o Create a short, memorable Twitter handle.
- o Ensure people can find you on Twitter using your handle and name.
- o Provide an appropriate profile picture.
- o Craft an approachable, keyword-rich bio.
- o Ensure that your background image and profile picture are the relevant dimensions.
- o Include relevant links in the link section under your bio.
- o Choose a tweet to pin to the top of your profile.
- o Remove anything offensive or unprofessional from your profile.

TWEETING

Tweeting the wrong sort of content is where many authors go wrong. Despite what you may believe, Twitter is not a shop full of buyers. Simply throwing out a link to your eBook page and saying, "Buy my book!" won't work. Believe me; in the early days, I tried and failed to get book sales that way. I think most people try this tactic possibly because they hear others praising Twitter and interpret that to mean that lots of followers equates to lots of easy sales. The reality couldn't be further from the truth.

This is what most people don't realise: Twitter won't sell books for you. If the only reason you want to get a big following on Twitter is to sell stuff to them today then this isn't the right book for you, and Twitter isn't the right platform. This may seem like an unpalatable plot twist. After all, you may ask yourself, "If you can't use it to sell books, why bother?" Hear me out. That doesn't mean that Twitter doesn't *lead* to sales and offer some tangible benefits. It just means you won't get quick sales by nagging your followers.

Users don't typically join Twitter to buy things. There's a certain degree of networking involved, but that shouldn't be your primary objective either. If you only want to network in a formal manner then maybe LinkedIn is better suited to your goals, as it's a site that has far more focus on business networking. What people on Twitter want is usually a combination of three things: entertainment, inspiration, and knowledge. Including at least one of these in every tweet will have a massive impact on your growth. I use a mixture of tweets to satisfy all three desires.

WHY TWEET AT ALL?

Twitter might not be an effective cold sales platform, but its potential is far more powerful. What it does is make you a personality, involving you in the lives of people who, after building a rapport with you, will trust you. Yes, this will make them more likely to buy your stuff but, more importantly, it will get them invested in your life and persuade them to help you in ways you could never imagine. That influence is far more powerful than making a quick buck.

Just ask YouTubers. Using their position as influencers with millions of trusting fans, they have used their following to push them onto bestsellers lists, get them onto offline chat shows, land them on music charts, and help them win competitions – not because they're great sales people, but because their fans care about them and will help them achieve some of the goals they set.

Helping others is a great way to gather initial support. For me, recommending blogs and retweeting my peers has stimulated reciprocal aid. At the same time, I started seeing an impact in the real world. Having met me on Twitter, readers across the world began checking out my fiction. I started being told that I've come up in conversations between people I've never met in countries I've never visited. English teachers have considered using my books as class texts. School pupils have recommended my work to their friends. As someone who is still a massive fan of the authors I was introduced to in my early teens, this is a very promising sign. It means that, by simply growing a following on Twitter and engaging with like-minded people, I have become someone they care about and want to see succeed.

Twitter's ability to drive traffic *en masse* is astounding. Over 100 people have started visiting my blog every day – and that number goes up to 500 visitors in a day when I occasionally post links to new content on Twitter. When I posted a short story on the story sharing website Wattpad, the audience I brought from Twitter impressed the Wattpad team so much that they offered to promote my story alongside a related movie advertising campaign. This resulted in my work gaining almost 30,000 reads in 70+ countries and led to additional sales of my other fiction.

Not only that, but my Twitter following has led to me being invited to events in the physical world. If people know you're an influencer, they want you to attend their events. Sometimes, they ask to feature you as a guest speaker. And that opens up an entirely new stream of income, as well as giving you new opportunities to sell your art to a new audience. You might not be able to sell books directly on Twitter but it can help you gain friends and influence people on a massive scale.

Your Twitter followers are not your customers: they're your army, a potentially limitless supply of soldiers who are willing to help you take over the world. "How do you build this force?" you might ask. Before we discuss specific things you could tweet that positively impact growth, I think it's best to start by telling you what engages Twitter users generally.

ENTERTAINMENT, INSPIRATION, KNOWLEDGE

For those seeking entertainment, I tweet jokes and give insights into my day-to-day life as an author. For followers who want inspiration, I talk about my projects and ambitions, and share news of my successes. And for those who seek knowledge – who are, in my case, often aspiring writers – I post links to blog posts I personally find informative.

Curating content in this way will later lead to your followers trusting your recommendations and following your links. This, as I have mentioned, can present itself as a powerful tool when it comes to requesting support.

Above all, remember to lace your tweets with positivity and intelligence. You may be used to ranting on your personal Facebook account, but on Twitter your aim should always be to present yourself professionally. If other users feel better after having read your tweets then you've made the right sort of impact. Before tweeting something new, always ask yourself, "Am I providing entertainment, inspiration, or knowledge?" If the answer is no then change the way you tweet. Once you've mastered the tone of your tweets, you can consider different ways in which you can use them to generate interest.

BEING CONTROVERSIAL

Likewise, when practicing your tone, you should also consider the demographic of your audience and the nature of the topics you tweet about. For example, if you are an author of erotic novels then your audience might be enticed by explicit description in your tweets. If you write religious books then your audience will unfollow you rapidly if you do this. If you're a punk rocker then your audience might expect your tweets to include swearing and attitude. A children's book illustrator using expletives will not go down so well with parents and teachers who might think you're setting a bad example for their children.

So much of mastering Twitter includes trying not to offend your followers. Filtering your thoughts and comments is key to maintaining the growth of your personal brand.

One major factor that often limits an individual's growth is discussing controversial topics online. By placing yourself on one side of an argument, you simultaneously alienate part of your audience and risk being unfollowed. This is why I recommend avoiding subjects like race, abortion, politics, and religion on social media. Discussing them almost always slows an account's growth. Clearly, this advice changes if your work is of a racial, political or otherwise controversial nature. Don't be too afraid to stand up for what you believe in but just don't go out of your way to make enemies.

I would definitely discourage arguing with other Twitter users, celebrities, or even internet trolls. The risk of showing yourself in a bad light far outweighs the possibility of winning an argument, even if you feel that you're in the right. Of course, there are always exceptions to this. Celebrity personalities like Jeremy Clarkson and Katie Hopkins are notorious for their offensive/controversial comments. They rose to the top for that reason and they maintain fame through their continued notoriety. For them, being infamous is their unique selling point.

However, as a creative professional, in general I would suggest that you stay away from controversy and let your art and originality speak for you.

PROFESSIONALISM & ERRORS

Having emphasised the importance of maintaining professionalism, I would suggest extending this attitude to the quality of writing on your profile as well as its subject. Too many times have I read the bios of self-titled "editors" with a spectacular lack of attention to detail, exposing glaring typos and bad grammar in their own writing. As a *professional* creative person, you should strive for professionalism in all aspects of your Twitter profile, especially if it relates directly to your job. Failing to do so can turn off potential followers who might lose interest when they spot your errors. In most cases, first impressions count.

There are no excuses for sloppy bios as they can be edited. When it comes to tweets, however, I realise that nobody is perfect. I have been guilty of the odd typo. Mistakes are natural, and tweets can't be edited once posted. If I spot one the moment I send a tweet then I delete it before anyone notices and quickly tweet a corrected version. If it's out and has been seen, however, it's best to leave it alone.

The nature of Twitter means that users write messages quickly. People will pick up on mistakes, especially if you're a writer, but you can simply shrug off occasional errors with a joke. They make you appear more human. Plus, crisis management can lead to unexpected hilarity and deepen comradery with your followers.

And, don't worry; even if the joke isn't funny, there are lots of different types of tweets that can help you make up for duds. Each has a unique power. We will explore the different types of tweets at your disposal. Now gear up! Next, we heading for the Twitter armoury!

TYPES OF TWEETS & HOW THEY GROW INFLUENCE

Now that you've mastered tone, tailoring your tweets for a specific demographic, and aiming to entertain, inspire, and provide knowledge, it's time to think about what *exactly* you're going to tweet.

As a creative person, you probably spend lots of time alone, writing a book, painting a canvas, or composing an album. You may think that this means you have little to talk about on social media. You may even wonder if you actually have enough to say to maintain an audience, let alone grown one. But don't worry; it's easier than it sounds.

I'm a prime example of how easy it is to maintain and grow a presence on Twitter as I've managed it for nearly four years. Admittedly, I now have more to talk about than I did at first, having released four books, run a publishing blog, and regularly attended literary events.

However, it hasn't always been that way. When I arrived at Twitter, I had no books, no blog, and rarely attended events. What I did have, however, was the focused aim of making a name for myself in the writing world, and the enthusiasm to maintain that focus. I also had enough of a grasp of English grammar to string together clear sentences and fit a thought into a single tweet – which, by the way, makes them more shareable.

Below, I've arranged a list of the types of tweets I've used during my time on Twitter. Some are basic and can be used to

37

gain a foothold on the ladder of influence. Others are a little more advanced and will be more effective once your following has grown.

By using some of the examples provided, you will learn how to maintain a buzz around you and your work, and I hope that you will realise that it's possible to find your voice even when you may feel like you have nothing to say at times.

SHARING YOUR DAY

The cliché of sharing messages about your everyday life may seem like a pointless exercise, but I'm starting with it because it works.

Its function is to familiarise your followers with you. By hearing about projects during their creation and seeing what you do to unwind, they experience your personality and become complicit in your success.

Yes, tweeting about food and everyday life can seem trivial, but showing an original perspective can help you stand out. For example, I don't talk about every meal I eat. I do, however, mention interesting meals that I have never tried before and discuss how I felt about them – a recent one being kangaroo steaks.

By showing your enthusiasm for something new, you share your discovery with the world. They get to experience your passion first hand, and it's infectious. If I talk about something I'm doing, I usually couple it with a profound comment or a joke to make it more worthy of engagement. There is a world of things to do out there. It's not the activity that matters; it's your enthusiasm, creative interpretation, and wit that makes it interesting. Examples of how I share my day include:

Putting away Christmas lights. What unsettles me more than the spider webs in the attic is that I can't see any spiders. #WhatGotTheSpiders

Planning a Route 66 adventure in a coffee shop with friends. 2800 miles in 18 days! NY, Chicago, Oklahoma, Amarillo, Vegas, & LA. #RoadTrip

Easter isn't Easter until you've threatened a chocolate egg with physical violence. Happy Easter! #ShutYourEggMouth

MAKING FRIENDS

After sharing a part of your day and seeing what others have been doing in your main feed, remember to engage in conversations. Don't just be passionate about your own life, be curious about others'. Reply to their tweets if they comment on yours.

Ask questions, give advice, or make jokes. A friendship isn't created by one person. If you want to build lasting relationships and maintain an active Twitter presence then you need to talk to people. The more interest you show in them, the more they'll show in you.

And don't worry about finishing conversations that have come to a natural end. That's where the "like" button comes in handy. It looks like a heart under every tweet that turns crimson when you click it. Using it is a great way to show that you've read a person's message without having to respond to everything all the time. Examples of how I reply to people include:

@AnthonyHorowitz Cool! When are they going to be released? I can't wait!

@tweetsunands Sorry, Sunanda. I don't mentor people. But I could suggest some useful writers' blogs if you're interested.

@whosthatkate You can do it, Katie! Just go to bed
early and set an alarm. I believe in you!

JOINING IN WITH SUCCESS

Success should be applauded. If you're a writer, this could
mean reaching your word count goal for the day. If you're a
musician, it could be playing to your biggest crowd ever or
recording a new song.

Sharing progress, no matter how small, is both
entertaining and inspirational. Likewise, if others have a book
signing or they survive a public speaking gig, congratulate
them. Your interest will make them want to continue to
progress and improve, and live up to your praise. It's all about
inspiring each other.

Just remember not to be self-deprecating. It can seem like
you're fishing for compliments. Count every bit of progress as a
success and be passionate about your achievements. This is
how I do it:

> @Keeneye214 That's awesome, Jeremy! It's great that
> you have a job that allows you to multi-task.
>
> Three strangers have now approached me to pre-order
> my new book, which wasn't even available for pre-
> order. One wanted the proof! #Promising
>
> A reader just contacted me to say that she named her
> new baby Toby - after the hero of my book
> #TheWinterFreakShow Wow!!!!!!

SETTING PUBLIC GOALS

If you're like me, you set yourself goals on a regular basis but
don't always achieve them. Publicly announcing your ambitions
to hundreds or thousands of Twitter followers can help you
succeed in this.

For me, the act often involves tweeting a daily word count goal or a book launch deadline. The fear of failing in front of everyone drives you to succeed. Of course, life sometimes gets in the way and you don't always end up with the result you were hoping for. Don't be afraid of this. In the case of most Twitter users, responses to these sorts of tweets, whether the artist is successful or not, are encouraging and supportive. And in some cases, other writers get involved, giving updates about their own progress for the day. Not only does it get your Twitter handle mentioned in more places and lead to more exposure, but it also provides you with the inspiration you need to continue your own work. I've set public deadlines like this:

> Only 2 days until I unveil the cover of my new fantasy book #Blott. Keep your eyes peeled! #AmWriting
>
> Finishing off the last proofread of my new novel #Blott. If all goes well, it should be launching on Amazon by the end of the day! #CantWait
>
> The final part of my comedy zombie story #Necroville comes out on Wattpad later, guys! Here's the story so far: https://www.wattpad.com/myworks/46973497-necroville

POSTING SNIPPETS OF YOUR WORK

This can be done whether you're a writer, musician, or artist. Whatever type of work you produce can be shared online.

For me, this often comes in the form of short quotes from whatever story I'm working on at the time. It will often be a line that I like, or something that I think expresses the tone of my current project. As an exercise for writers, this can be useful as you will often find that your favourite quotes don't fit into one tweet. By fine-tuning them so that they fit, you will simultaneously be tailoring ready-made marketing material for when the book is released. And that's a massive advantage in a world where people love to share quotes from J. K. Rowling and Dr. Seuss.

Besides increasing your shareability, posting snippets of your work also plugs gaps in your Twitter stream when you haven't done anything in the real world that's worth tweeting about. After all, everyone has boring days, but as an artist you have an advantage over everyone else; you create things. You might have had a boring day, but your characters could be fighting for their lives! If you're a musician or painter, you can easily share your work in a similar way by tweeting out a riff or an early painting concept.

At the very least, you can use this tactic to evaluate the popularity of ideas. If you tweet out a quote or idea that is amazing, your followers will tell you. Whereas if you tweet something that's much blander on paper than it seemed in your head, a lack of interaction on that tweet will tell you that it needs revising. As a creator, sharing what you love to do is useful in so many ways. There's a reason why people watch behind-the-scenes footage of shows and films: they love to see the creation process. Here are some examples of how I share my work:

> Just invented a word. "Unsnuffable." It's going in the first draft of my new story. If Shakespeare can do it then so can I. #AmWriting

Daniel Parsons
@dkparsonswriter

A description of a character I just introduced in my new book. Villains are so fun to write! #AmWriting #NaNoWriMo

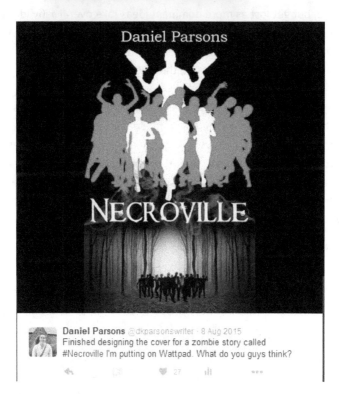

"Every part of his clothing was a different animal, like he had fallen into a hunter's trophy cabinet and re-emerged cloaked in death."

Daniel Parsons

NECROVILLE

Daniel Parsons @dkparsonswriter · 8 Aug 2015
Finished designing the cover for a zombie story called #Necroville I'm putting on Wattpad. What do you guys think?

43

SURREAL COMEDY & DAYDREAMS

Just because you've given yourself a day off work as a creator, that doesn't mean your mind has had a day off dreaming up new concepts and ideas. Every creative person's imagination is constantly working, gathering inspiration from things around them.

The same goes for me. As an author, how many of these ideas can I turn into full stories? Probably only a small proportion of them. Most of the concepts that spring into my mind only stay there for a few minutes because they amuse me, but get lost as more dominant ideas take over. Many ideas I have either don't fit the style of my creative work, or I think they're fun but doubt that their novelty would last the course of an entire book. As a result, they would usually be wasted.

Until Twitter.

On my days off, I use these random – normally useless – thoughts to show a little bit of my personality on Twitter. You may call me odd, but every writer needs a streak of weirdness to make them original. Some of the following tweets have served me very well in the past, showing me that my weirdest thoughts are often the ones that my followers relate to most:

> "Alright, I'll just have one piece of chocolate."
> *Wakes up 3 days later in a skip, 35 stone, with a Mike Tyson face tattoo.*

> Just found a millipede in my wardrobe. Now I'm searching the rest of my bedroom for the married millipede whose husband came home early.

> What if prize-winning flowers and vegetables at gardening festivals are actually viewed as morbidly obese by other plants?

Tweeting in this way may seem frivolous but it actually makes you more appealing to follow as people appreciate random and original humour. It's certainly more fun than scrolling over banal breakfast photos and sales pitches from strangers.

In some cases, this type of tweet catches your followers' imaginations and they elaborate on your joke. The entertainment factor makes your account appealing to follow and your tweets easy to share. Once your followers like you, they will be more willing to listen to the serious things you want to say.

ASKING QUESTIONS & ADVISE

I often like to get a second opinion on my ideas. Tweeting ideas to followers is an effective way to get instant feedback before deciding to dedicate further time to writing a scene of questionable value. The same can go for song titles or the theme of a painting.

Obviously, you don't have to let your followers' views steer your work in ways you don't want it to go, but gauging a general consensus of opinion can be a handy indicator of which ideas work well and which ones you might want to scrap before wasting any more time on them.

I have also used this method when encountering specific editing problems that I couldn't easily solve alone. Posting a line of your work and asking for editing advice can be extremely helpful, especially if you're followed by a lot of experienced people in your field.

If you do go down the route of tweeting ideas, don't worry about them being stolen. Even if your followers love an idea and say that they wish they had thought of it, they're unlikely to steal it. Few people have the time to explore their own ideas, never mind steal yours.

CROWD PLEASERS

Crowd pleasers are tweets that gather easy retweets as they appeal to your typical follower. They are often either funny or frivolous messages that you know will be popular with your audience. These may go on to be used as your pinned tweet for that constant trickle of retweets I mentioned earlier. An example of a crowd pleaser is:

> The key to success is acting like you know what you're doing until you actually know what you're doing.
> Unless you're a surgeon…

Firstly, it works well because it adheres to two of the three key aims of any tweet, offering inspiration and entertainment. Secondly, it appeals my followers' nature of being hard-working optimists which means that it's more likely to be retweeted. As a result I used it as my pinned tweet for several months, a move which generated hundreds of retweets and likes, as well as a boost in my follower numbers.

Other crowd pleasers I have used have included the themes of reading and writing – common interests among my followers and the people who follow them in turn. As a creative person it's usually easy to figure out what types of tweets will appeal to your target audience. Here are some more examples:

> In a possible future, some kid is using your story as inspiration to follow their dreams. Don't let that kid down! #MotivationMonday

> Many readers don't know the importance of reviewing authors' books online. Just a few lines could change your favourite writer's life. #MotivationMonday

Once you know what topics you can rely on for success, you can create your own crowd pleasers.

Trending Tweets

Many trends on Twitter start out small and localised, often initiated by a single act or picture, and then spiral into global talking points. Ordinary people who never sought fame often trend worldwide on Twitter.

An example of this is a teenage boy from the United States. His name was Alex Lee and he worked in the American supermarket chain Target. A teenage girl took a photo of him folding clothes and posted it on Twitter, commenting on how attractive she found him. Within hours, adolescent girls from all over the world retweeted his picture and discussed his identity, discovering his name, age, and home town. Soon, #AlexFromTarget was trending worldwide and his Twitter account (@AlexLeeWorld) grew in popularity. Within two weeks he had amassed 750,000 followers, appeared on Ellen Degeneres' hit talk show, and was offered lucrative endorsement deals. Although this initial surge of worldwide fame wasn't maintained, some of it has remained as he now has a successful YouTube channel and a tribe of avid followers.

Attracting curiosity levels like this is not something that can be replicated intentionally. Alex Lee rose to fame through pure luck. I'm not saying everyone can achieve the same feat. However, with a bit of social media know-how, anyone can grow into a social juggernaut over a long period of time. They are just unlikely to see massive overnight success.

Viral tweets can happen at any time to anyone. Here are two examples of ones that got unexpected momentum, the first spurring an infamous Twitter scandal, and the second being the most retweeted tweet ever:

Justine Sacco
@JustineSacco

Going to Africa. Hope I don't get AIDS. Just
kidding. I'm white!

← Reply ⟲ Retweet ☆ Favorite ••• More

3,172   **1,505**
RETWEETS   FAVORITES

Ellen DeGeneres ✓
@TheEllenShow   ⚙ ⚐ Follow

If only Bradley's arm was longer. Best photo
ever. #oscars

RETWEETS   LIKES
3,342,332 2,157,127

Trending tweets can have two very different outcomes.
While Twitter gave Alex Lee a career in entertainment and
boosted Ellen's career drastically, it also ruined Justine Sacco's
life, taking away her job in public relations and making her the
recipient of global hatred. If you're hoping for your tweets to
go viral, make sure they trend for the right reasons by thinking
about your tweets before you send them.

TWEETS FOR LARGER ACCOUNTS

Some more advanced tweet options become available to you as your online presence grows. Having more followers means that more avid fans will be online at any one time, ready to engage with your tweets.

Creative professionals can often use the following types of tweet to see unprecedented results, both in online exposure and in real-world networking. The tactics I'm about to show you are incredibly powerful, but I'd caution you to be selective and use them sparingly. Resorting to these types of tweet too often can come across as demanding to your followers, a move that results in decreased interaction over time. If used correctly, these tweets can massively increase your online and offline influence.

VOTING

As your follower count grows, you will find that you increasingly have the scope to gauge a consensus of their opinions. Obtaining these opinions can help you make informed creative decisions. It's free market research.

For example, many indie authors use this tactic when picking a new book cover from several potential options. Instead of just picking whichever one they like, they put up the choices on Twitter and get their followers to vote for their favourite.

Using this method can give you a better idea of what your fans are more likely to buy and so it can directly improve your sales. Users who voted will also feel like they contributed to the creation process and that their opinions matter. Involving them generates interest in the end product and turns your followers into collaborators.

While it's true that nobody cares about a project as much as its creator, what this form of complicit marketing does is generate a legion of fans who come to see your project as their baby too, and they want to see it succeed. It's also fun to see the buzz this method generates before a project has officially been released.

Previously, the way many people used to poll their followers was to set up two or more competing hashtags on any particular topic and then get people to tweet their opinions about them, using those hashtags. The originator of the hashtag could gage the popularity of conflicting choices based on the amount of times each hashtag was used, and the qualitative comments attached to each hashtag. Through this process, a general opinion was formed. (For more information on this method, look at the section on Hashtag Voting.)

More recently, Twitter has innovated the way you can tweet so that you can track the results of a poll more easily without having to look at individual tweets from lots of different accounts. All you have to do is write the question you want to ask in the body of your tweet and then click the "poll" button at the bottom of the tweet window. This will make the whole process easier and will lead to considerably more contributors – as many as ten times more in my experience! Here's a poll I launched recently:

Daniel Parsons
@dkparsonswriter

Just got asked to launch more of my ebooks as paperbacks before a book festival in September. What do you guys read?

23% eBooks

77% Print Books

335 votes • Final results

RETWEETS 7   LIKES 28

It got 335 votes and 25 replies. Despite this, I would still recommend occasionally trying the old method of asking people to write their opinions rather than hitting a vote button because it has more indirect benefits.

Let me explain. Firstly, with the new polls nobody repeats your hashtags, so the chance of getting your tweet trending is dramatically reduced. Secondly, staging an automatic poll prioritises votes over unique input from your followers. It gives two or more options and asks people to pick one, when their preferred answer might actually be that a mixture of the options is best, or some other option not listed. Prioritising a numerical voting system over open debate means that you could lose valuable input that would otherwise arise. This might make your followers feel less involved in your work and could lead to them becoming less active in your questions. I would work my way around this issue by asking people to vote in the form of comments, using the words or hashtags I have provided. If I did it using the previous example, I would word it like this:

> Thinking about releasing my books in more formats.
> #Paperbacks Vs #eBooks. What do you guys read and
> why? #Vote

Encouraging your followers to argue a case for their choice gets them even more invested in your work. Sometimes they even debate with each other in the comment section of your original tweet. The extra mentions will get your debate more word-of-mouth exposure and will thus spread your influence further. Plus, it will possibly raise issues in your work that you might never have considered. Using this method rather than the simple poll requires a little more work but it has many extra benefits.

BETTER THAN GOOGLE

Tweeting questions to your followers is a great way to get a consensus of opinion on a subject to help you make quick, informed decisions based on instant feedback from the very people who are likely to buy your work. As your following grows, your ability to get a views grows with it.

This approach can also be applied to getting facts. In my experience Twitter can be a far better search engine than Google. For example, I once needed to know something specific about copyright law. In a book I wrote, one of my characters sang the lyrics from a well-known Christmas song. What concerned me was whether I was legally allowed to use the lyrics in this context. A Google search told me that the rights to the song were owned by a large company, so the lyrics were definitely copyrighted. However, when searching copyright law, I found that copyrighted lyrics *could* be used under certain circumstances. After spending hours trawling blog posts and legal websites I couldn't find out whether or not I was allowed to use them. That was when I decided to tweet my question to my followers. Within an hour I had received more than twenty responses from authors and lawyers who had real-life experience of this specific issue. Between them, they gave me the correct answer as well as providing me with links to credible online resources that backed up their arguments.

This reaction surprised me. What surprised me more was that, although some of my followers didn't know the answer, they knew people who might. One of them even brought into the discussion the bestselling crime author Ian Rankin who pointed the debate in the right direction.

What we can take from this example is that growing a large and active Twitter following can offer you informed expertise, valuable opinions, and credible experience that a search engine can never deliver. It makes logical sense. After all, when you're followed by thousands of people then the chances that one of them knows the thing you need to know is pretty high. And in a world where you often need information quickly to make decisions, having an army of experts at your disposal can mean the difference between blundering into a crisis and expertly dancing around it.

NETWORKING

Have you ever turned up to an event, like a festival or a craft fair, and not known how to introduce yourself to prospective contacts? I can fully empathise with you if you've felt this way. Events can be overwhelming, especially if you don't know anyone there. Sometimes, you can find yourself wandering around the venue aimlessly without actually getting involved in any networking. Luckily, Twitter can help with this and make you a networking pro.

From the very beginning of my Twitter experience I have used my account to network online, using my online influence to attract writers to my blog as well as interacting with experts in my field as though they were my personal mentors. I have built up online relationships that have led to overseas book sales, and I have learned about things from other cultures that I could not possibly have known without talking to people on Twitter.

The process of creating relationships with other professionals can be extended to organising real-world meetups. I originally encountered this idea through Joanna Penn, a bestselling author who has used the following process to build strong links with key players in her industry.

How it works is simple.

It starts by using Twitter to search for people who are attending events that you also plan to attend. This is a relatively easy task due to the searchability of words and hashtags associated with most events.

For example, many authors and publishers use book fairs to network. One of the biggest is the London Book Fair. In the build-up to their 2016 event, the London Book Fair's organisers used the hashtag #LBF16 to help track their programme of events and visitor attendance. By clicking on the #LBF16 hashtag and scrolling down its feed, you can find other people who are going to be attending as well. This same process can be used to discover attendees of comic book conventions, art exhibitions, music festivals, etc. in just the same way.

Once you have discovered relevant professionals that are going to be attending the same event as you, tweet them, introducing yourself and suggesting a location and time to meet with them during the event. When you arrive, this prior introduction helps you to start conversations with people you follow and respect without the need of being introduced. Twitter's open access to celebrities and influencers has revolutionised this process, eradicating the need for a mutual friend in order to meet the people you want to work with most.

Alternatively, you could just tweet out a public invitation, advertising a specific location and time where you will be waiting to meet other event attendees. This works best if you have lots of followers and don't mind who you meet.

Obviously, there are problems with this tactic. The first is that none of your followers might be attending that event. Retweets can help you to overcome this issue, extending your reach to Twitter users who may be attending.

Include the event's official hashtag in your tweets about the event, so that other people at the event who are following the hashtag will be able to see it. This will help to get your invitation in front of the right people.

Your second problem is the people who join you might not be the type you wanted to meet. This may seem like a waste of time, but at least you will have done some networking, which was possibly more than you were doing before you tweeted about the impromptu meetup. Just meeting a few people at an event and learning their names can boost your confidence, possibly enough to approach bigger players you may still want to meet.

Try using Twitter to network. Even if nobody responds to your tweet invitation, others following the event's hashtag may follow you. Either way, it's a great way to increase your influence in your field. You never know, you might successfully network *and* grow your following.

LIVE-TWEETING YOUR EVENTS

The beauty of Twitter is that you can host an event from the comfort of your own home without ever having to organise a venue. This is a virtual event.

I've used this tactic several times, hosting a writing marathon I call #Writeathon, to great effect. During #Writeathon I invite other writers to get involved. I usually start these events with an interactive call-to-action like this:

> About to start a #Writeathon - writing 5000 words in one day. Who's with me? Join in or support others. Just get involved in #Writeathon

All you have to do is create an original hashtag for your event and then live-tweet about it throughout the day. Your followers can easily follow the event as it unfolds, using your hashtag. If they want to get involved then all they have to do is comment on it, including the same hashtag.

#Writeathon – a 5,000-word writing marathon I host frequently – is my most successful virtual event to date. I start by tweeting about it the day before the event. That gives people who want to get involved just enough time to clear their schedule, but not so much time that they forget it's happening. On the morning of the big day I start by announcing my word count goal – or some other measurable objective – and then I tweet updates about my progress as the day progresses. What tends to happen with an event like this is that you get a swell of interaction at the start of the day. Some followers will wish you luck, while others offer advice and encouragement for staying on track. Some might get involved and try to race you to the finish line.

At the end of your event, when you reach your goal, you'll

usually experience a boost in comments and retweets as your followers congratulate you and share your success to inspire others, or share their own experience.

And it doesn't just have to be a writing event. You could live-tweet a charity fundraiser, or an art auction, or a Kickstarter campaign. As long as you have something you can share progress on throughout the day, the event's topic doesn't really matter.

Hosting a virtual event is an effective way to be seen as an authority in your field. Follower participation will increase your influence and reach, as well as helping you to share an insight into your creative process with your followers. Live-tweeting events is one of Twitter's strengths, making it superior to other social media platforms for interactivity. If you use live-tweeting to maximum effect, you could even find your event trending globally, leading to a whole new level of exposure.

How Often Should I Tweet?

Deciding on how frequently you should tweet depends entirely on what you have to say and whether or not you're contributing to a live event. The average tweet has a 45-minute lifespan, with the majority of interactions happening in its first 15 minutes. Because of that short window, it's acceptable to tweet the same information several times per day without being considered a spammer. However, you should definitely prioritise quality over quantity. Yes, you may have to reply to lots of people, but the handful of original tweets you broadcast each day should always follow the three rules of Twitter etiquette: entertain, inspire, or provide knowledge, or a combination of the three.

I've seen Twitter accounts with over a million followers

that have under three interactions (retweets, likes, or comments) per tweet. As they tweet dozens of times per day, nobody seems to be paying any attention to what they have to say. Obviously, this is bad.

I tend to tweet approximately two or three times per day, plus I reply to people who comment on my tweets. It's okay to miss the occasional day, and sometimes reply to lots of tweets in one sitting – maybe as many as thirty if you've fallen behind – but these extremes don't occur often for me as I try to keep my activity consistent, sending no more than ten replies in one sitting.

For each of my original tweets, I aim for quality interactions over a quantity of tweets. A good indicator of that is to achieve upwards of one interaction for every 3,000 followers you have. So if you have 9,000 followers, you should look for at least three retweets, likes, or comments for each of your tweets. Remember: you want actions. Impressions alone don't count for everything.

That should give you an idea of how active you should be. You won't tweet as often when you first get started but, as your account grows, your tweets will get more responses and you will find yourself getting involved in more conversations.

Don't worry if you have fewer than 3,000 followers at the moment. This doesn't mean that you won't get any interactions. It just means that you probably won't get interactions on *every* tweet. All you need is one retweet from someone with considerably more followers than you and that could change overnight.

There will come a point when you can't respond to everyone individually. When that happened to me, I cut down on responding to generic "thank you for the follow" messages, and ended meaningless conversations early by liking a comment to show that I agree without dragging out the conversation any further. This meant that I could spend more time working on my books and delivering quality content.

Using your own judgment is good practice. After all, you can't spend your entire day tweeting. It would distract you from the work you're ultimately trying to promote. Artists create. As long as you neither tweet endlessly nor completely abandon Twitter, you should be fine.

PROTECTED TWEETS

bravo 🔒
If FOLLOWS YOU
r.animador.fotógrafo.Dj.

@bravollajadj's Tweets are protected.

Only confirmed followers have access to @bravollajadj's Tweets and complete profile
Click the "Follow" button to send a follow request

In your Twitter settings, you will have the option to make your tweets available for public viewing or available only to those who you allow access. If your tweets are protected then people who view your profile will see a locked padlock symbol next to your name on your profile and won't be able to follow you until after you have manually approved them. Protecting your tweets may sound like a good idea if you're afraid of being trolled (harassed by malicious accounts), but the risk of this happening is minimal. Even if it does happen, you can simply make your tweets invisible to selected accounts by blocking them.

I recommend not protecting your tweets. This way, people won't be irritated by having to request permission to view them, if they bother to ask at all. Not only will it generate more follower growth but it also means that your account will be visible in more places and conversations. In turn, more people will be given the opportunity to follow you.

Maintaining Replies

Making every tweet a big hit is great, but successful tweets can create vast amounts of traffic on your profile which can become overwhelming if you don't deal with it effectively. Falling behind on responding can mean missing opportunities and breaking relationships you would rather strengthen. In the worst case scenario, people could forget about you or interpret your tardiness as ignorance and decide not to bother commenting on your tweets again.

Keeping up can be a real challenge, particularly if you have active supporters. It only takes a day or two of not replying to comments to create a backlog that keeps getting bigger the longer you put it off. I've always found keeping up with replies difficult but I try to respond to most comments, even if it takes a few days to tackle the backlog. The problem with letting your notifications build up is that Twitter has installed a cut-off point where you're unable to scroll back through notifications further than a few days. If you value the input of you followers then you can see why this could cause an issue. Taking a break for too long could mean losing some messages forever.

Luckily, you can filter your notifications to save vital minutes scrolling and also give yourself a few extra days to catch up with replies without losing comments. When you click on "Notifications" in Twitter's top panel, to look at the interactions your tweets have received, you are given two options; you can either look at "Notifications," meaning all interactions including comments, retweets, and likes, or you can look at "Mentions" which only includes comments. Switching from "Notifications" to the more streamlined "Mentions" stream enables you to scroll back several days further, giving you the information you need to reply to older comments. Although this switch doesn't work on mobile devices, it can be particularly helpful if you go on a long break and don't have time to reply to comments during your travels as you can catch up on messages when you get home.

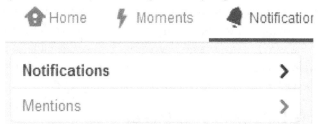

OPTIMISING YOUR TWEETS

When raising awareness of an event in the real world, many people hand out flyers to advertise it. Lots of inner city nightclubs often hire teams of students to hand out thousands of leaflets to promote a guest DJ. The problems for creative professionals is that it's costly to do this for a book signing, gallery exhibition, or music gig. Not only does it take a huge effort to get the coverage you want, but there are printing costs and wages to be paid. And even after that, most people will just throw away the leaflet as it doesn't appeal to them.

This is where Twitter can help. How many leaflets could you hand out in a day? 100? 500? 2,000? Think of how much they cost to print and how many people actually read them. On Twitter you have an active audience. Yes, it's true that not all of your followers will read your tweets, but if you've grown your account wisely, you should have a high number of interested supporters. Posting a tweet instead of handing out flyers saves you time and money, plus a long stint in the harsh weather. It's free and could be done quickly while you're at home waiting for the kettle to boil.

Of course, ensuring that you optimise your posts to reach the most people takes some tinkering as your followers will most likely live in many different time zones, but it's still a lot easier than handing out flyers. I've tested tweeting at different times of the day so I can reach more people and avoid tweeting at the worst times, thereby increasing my interaction level per tweet. You'd be surprised by how many more people get involved in your events this way!

THE LIFE SPAN OF A TWEET

I've mentioned that an average tweet has a 45-minute lifespan, with the bulk of interactions happening in the first 15 minutes. What this means is that timing is crucial when it comes to ensuring that every one of your tweets is successful, especially if you have an international audience.

When testing tweets on my own followers at different times of the day, I discovered that I tend to get more response in the evening (UK time). This is probably because 55% of my followers live in the US, meaning that most of them are fast asleep until about noon in the UK.

You can easily find out the most common nationalities of your followers by looking into your followers' stats on Twitter's "Analytics" page. Along with running some tests of your own, this information will help you maximise the power of your tweets by reaching more of your followers in the 45-minute window when your tweet is active.

MAKING EVERY TWEET A BIG HIT

This, however, is just the beginning when it comes to

optimising your tweets. I've seen Twitter "experts" mention timing on their blogs. What I've never seen mentioned, however, is what I am about to tell you – a trick that cranks up a Tweet's impact beyond what is naturally possible. The idea involves attracting an abnormal amount of targeted traffic to your Twitter profile at the time you post an important tweet.

I do this almost daily and my interactions have exploded since I discovered this technique. It's really quite simple. All you have to do is synchronise the types of people you follow with what you're tweeting. It takes some planning but what you will find is that the number of followers you gain, and the scale of interactions you get, will both be boosted by putting this idea into practice.

Let's discuss an example to explain properly how to do this. After a day of editing a manuscript I might tweet some amusing observation or tip about the editing process. After that, I'll use ManageFlitter Pro's Power Mode to search for accounts that fit into my normal follow criteria, focusing specifically on people whose bios include the word "editor." I'll then follow several hundred editors. One of the first things they'll do is look at my profile and notice that my most recent tweet talks about editing. As they are the ideal demographic for the subject, they're more likely to relate to me and hit the follow button, as well as retweet, like, or comment on the tweet itself. Repeating this strategy for different types of people will maintain a high level of interactions on your tweets every day.

The process can be applied to any subject:

1. Tweet about a subject or event.
2. Follow lots of people who have shown an interest in that subject or event.
3. See an increased level of follows and interactions.

The strategy doesn't have to use key words in people's bios, either. You can also achieve the same level of punch by searching key words in people's tweets, as long as those keywords identify their interests accurately. I tend to use hashtags to ensure a degree of relevance.

CONSIDER DEVICES & THEIR IMPACT

Thinking about the device on which your tweets will be read can help you boost your tweets' potential lifespans and interactions. Not everyone uses Twitter on a laptop. Many people – particularly younger users – use the internet primarily on their smartphone. The browsing experience on these devices is considerably different to a desktop or laptop.

When you click on someone's Twitter profile on a computer, their tweet feed is shown down the middle of the screen, presenting only their original tweets. All replies to comments are automatically filtered out unless you click the "Tweets & Replies" button at the top. However, on a smartphone those replies are left unfiltered by default.

As a result, a brilliant tweet you posted only a few hours ago could go unseen by lots of followers who visit your profile if you've replied to a lot of comments since tweeting it. To combat this problem, you could post your original tweets *after* you've posted your string of replies. That way you can harvest extra interactions from mobile device users by making it easier for them to see your best tweets at the top of your feed. This makes for an adequate replacement for your pinned tweet – which doesn't show up on mobile devices – and makes you more effective when it comes to engaging with followers who use mobile devices.

SUMMARY

The example tweets provided here are just some ideas of creative things you can do on Twitter to maintain your activity and provide a more fruitful user experience. Accounts that are consistently active (but not excessively so) tend to gain more interaction so this section should give you some idea of how to optimise your content.

The key is to tweet frequently enough to make yourself recognisable to your followers – without clogging up their feeds and desensitising them to your words.

If used correctly, this armoury of tweets – from the very basic to the most advanced – will ensure that you never run out of things to say on Twitter. Just remember the mantra: entertainment, inspiration, knowledge. These are the keys to your content.

TWEETING CHECKLIST

In summary, you should:

- o Ensure all tweets strengthen your brand.
- o Tweet varied content that addresses the three basic principles of good tweets.
- o Avoid tweeting about controversial subjects unless being controversial matches your brand.
- o Ensure your tweets have no errors before sending them.
- o Make quick judgements about whether or not to delete a tweet that you have noticed contains errors, depending on its early interactions.
- o Vary the types of tweets you broadcast so that they match your immediate and long-term aims.
- o Aim to get your tweets trending.
- o Experiment with online networking, conducting polls, and live-tweet your events.
- o Tweet often enough to remind your followers that you exist but not so often that your tweets get ignored.
- o Ensure your account settings are set to "public" so strangers can see your tweets.
- o Reply to your followers' comments.
- o Follow my process of making every tweet a big hit.
- o Adapt your tweeting habits to ensure success on both computers and mobile devices.

ADDING MEDIA
TO YOUR TWEETS

Using media in your tweets involves any content other than plain text. This can come in the form of an image, a video, a link, or an animated gif, which is a short silent video that loops continuously.

Including media can drastically change the level of interaction your tweets attract, both for the better and for worse. There's no hard-and-fast rule when it comes to adding content as you have to take into account the aim of each tweet and its intended audience.

For example, elderly people who use a desktop computer may experience Twitter differently to teens who are more likely to view the mobile version. As a result, the tweets you send out may appear very differently to each type of user. Choosing the right type of media can determine an individual tweet's success, so you should consider how your tweet will look on different devices before sending it.

"Fine! I'll just tweet without using media at all. Surely my words are enough?" I hear you say.

Well, not necessarily. You see, you don't just have to take into account the tweet's audience. You also have to consider the social situation in which your tweet is going to be seen.

For example, a comment discussing a video that has gone viral might perform better with the video attached as it provides it for those people who haven't seen it yet. Whereas a comment without the video might get drowned out by other tweets that provide context to their comments. This example specifically refers to cases found on a trending hashtag feed where people might click on the hashtag to find out what the buzz is all about. In that situation, they're more likely to interact with the tweets that educate them first by showing them what is attracting all the attention.

HOW TO INCLUDE MEDIA IN YOUR TWEETS

You can include media by clicking on the camera icon at the bottom left-hand corner of the window where you write a tweet. Alternatively, a relatively new "gif" button has been installed to the right of it. You can use this to search for appropriate gifs from the internet.

Any media you include in the tweet will not take up any of your 140 characters but media will still be presented as a link for mobile users to click on and view.

In most cases you would use media to include extra meaning to your tweets. Many people use images that include whole paragraphs of text on them to extend the 140 characters available. I would discourage this sloppy approach unless it's absolutely necessary as most good tweets work best when edited to fit into the 140 characters permitted. If you include an image with text, consider using memes (highly shareable images overlaid with brief text). Their brevity often makes them more amusing.

A more effective way to use media involves adding a visual element to your tweet text for maximum impact. This will include content that is designed to deliver one of the three fundamental tweet aims: entertainment, inspiration, or knowledge.

For entertainment, you could use media to provide a punchline to a joke you included in the body of a tweet. As inspiration, the attachment could display someone achieving something extraordinary, thus emphasising your tweet's motivational tone. Or the media could provide a graph or teaching aid that helps to demonstrate knowledge.

Adding media to tweets often helps them to stand out as they clarify meaning. Plus, they often take up more room on people's screens, becoming more of a focal point in their feed. See for yourself. Check out any trending hashtag and you'll find that some of the highest performing tweets include media.

Let's look at each of the three different types of media you can add to a tweet, and their place on Twitter. The first one is the humble picture.

1. USING PICTURES ON TWITTER

Pictures can be uploaded as JPEG, PNG, and GIF files. These are the most common forms of media you will find attached to tweets.

I often like to use striking images as long as they provide appropriate entertainment, inspiration, or knowledge. If the body of your tweet is about fitness and what you've achieved at the gym then you might include an inspirational quote and a picture of a striving athlete. If you make a joke about something that's trending, then the body of you tweet may be dry and sarcastic but the image can provide a visual punchline to show that your words are meant in good humour.

Pictures are extremely popular on Twitter. If you're contributing to a trending hashtag, then utilising an image is a great way to draw attention away from the multitude of similar tweets and gain more interactions – providing the tweet is of a good quality and the image enhances the text. Including an image for the sole purpose of taking up more space will get you nowhere.

There is little difference in the level of interaction amongst old or young users, or even between devices when it comes to using tweets that include images. Desktop users don't have to do anything to expand a tweet and mobile users seem to be comfortable clicking on links on their handheld device to view extra content.

Images are probably the best place to start when

experimenting with media in tweets as they are the simplest form to use and they generally perform well.

2. ANIMATED GIFs

GIFs are picture files that can be static images but can also be used as short, silent videos that play on a continuous loop. They are actually an image file, rather than a video file, so they load faster and play on more devices than video file formats. Including them in your tweets is one of Twitter's most recent innovations and has allowed for a ton of extra creativity from its users.

Animated GIFs can be hit and miss in terms of impact. Given the right conditions, they can provide more visual clout than single images, but they can also fail to load for users with a slow internet connection. Due to their looping nature, they tend to portray characters in a humorous and erratic way, meaning that they can often be used for comedic effect.

I've used this type of media myself, following the announcement of an upcoming sequel to a popular animated movie. To show my excitement, I used a gif in which one of the characters from the original movie was wild with enthusiasm at seeing bubbles, mentioning that he looked like me at the moment the trailer for the new movie was released.

This tweet hit several criteria for success. Not only was it funny, but it contributed to a trending hashtag, which got additional exposure. Plus, my followers who had seen the original movie got the inside joke and felt a sense of comradery.

3. VIDEOS

It is possible to use videos of any length and resolution on Twitter. If you include a video as a link to a video-sharing site like YouTube then the video will embed into your tweet and can be viewed on Twitter. Alternatively, you can record the video live on a phone and upload it that way.

Facebook recently took up the mantle from YouTube as the world's largest video-sharing website. It's true that posts that contain videos on Facebook gain high levels of engagement when compared to other types of posts. Despite the success of videos on Facebook, this success hasn't transferred to Twitter. When it comes to social media platforms, each one is a different beast, with different interfaces, and dissimilar users. What works for one won't automatically work across them all.

On Twitter I've found that videos have the potential to gain massive levels of engagement when given the right conditions. Those conditions, however, rarely occur because they include delivering the news *before* mainstream broadcasters, being the original poster of a viral video, or having a large existing fan base who know you for your video content on sites like YouTube or Vine.

None of these scenarios are easy to accomplish. For the first two you have to be in the right place at the right time to capture videos that have the potential to go viral – impossible to achieve regularly, if at all. And for the final scenario you have to have already built a substantial audience (on a video-sharing platform like YouTube or Vine) who will look for your video content on Twitter. For everyone else on Twitter, video media still lags behind images and animated GIFs in terms of engagement.

Of course this could all change – that's the nature of social media. I add this caveat because Twitter has recently released a new app called Periscope which is a video-sharing service that focuses on smartphones. Videos uploaded there are only available for a short time, and they can only be watched by people who use Twitter. Evidently, Twitter is trying to replicate the success of its more video-based competitors in order to grow its market share.

The main thing to remember is that you need to consider the demographic of a tweet's audience and the situation in which it's going to be viewed. However, with innovations happening every day, I would highly recommend that you continue to experiment.

MEDIA CHECKLIST

In summary, you should:

o   Post at least one tweet that contains media every week.

o   Experiment with media forms by including pictures, gifs, and videos in your tweets.

o   Find out what types of media work best for you and use them more often in your tweets.

RETWEETING

Retweets are the Twitter equivalent of sharing on Facebook, or re-pinning on Pinterest. If your tweet is retweeted then not only will your followers be able to see it, but the followers of the person who retweeted it will also see it. Getting retweeted by lots of people can expand your audience dramatically. Even getting retweeted by one person with lots of followers can make a big difference.

You can retweet other people's tweets in two ways. Which way you choose alters who gets credit for the tweet. Claiming credit matters on Twitter as it directly affects your Klout score which measures your online influence. I'll discuss Klout in more detail further into this book. For the purpose of this section all you need to know is that it's important, particularly if you live in the United States.

To retweet something that you find interesting or funny, the easiest way to do so is to click the retweet button under the original tweet.

It looks like a loop made of two arrows and will turn green when you've clicked it. What this means is that the original tweet will be presented on your Twitter feed and will be shared with all of your followers. As far as claiming credit for any future retweets and favourites the tweet gets after you have retweeted it, this is where the situation gets complicated.

If you retweet something without altering it then you only receive credit for retweets that arise directly from *your* retweet. So you will only get credit if your followers retweet the tweet you shared. The credit for any retweets your followers get from their followers goes only to them and the original poster, not to you.

However, you can claim more credit for yourself by adding content to the retweet. When you hit the retweet button, Twitter will offer you the opportunity to add your own comment to the original tweet. This alteration arrived in 2015 and allows people to give their own perspective to another person's tweet while also sharing the original message with their followers. By doing this, you essentially create a new tweet that contains the original one. Instead of having the original poster's profile picture attached to the tweet, it will now show yours. This gives you credit for any retweets you get from *your* followers but also gives you credit for future retweets from *their* followers – as long as they don't add their own comment.

This tactic may seem underhanded but in many cases it can help the original poster, particularly if the way they initially tweeted the information wasn't particularly retweet-friendly. They may have posted a good link that offers information but it may not have received much interaction due to them writing a bland description. By adding a witty or humorous comment onto the tweet, you could make it far more shareable. As a result, the original poster's words would be shown in a more desirable light, improving their public profile. The only cost to them is losing out on some third-party retweets.

I have done this a few times. One instance was when a renowned indie author posted a link to a blog post alongside a dry description. I retweeted it and added a joke of my own to make it more shareable. As a result, my tweet got more interactions than the original tweet despite me having fewer followers than the famous author.

This is how a retweet with a comment looks after it has been posted:

RETWEETING EVENTS

Here is an example to show you how you can get great interaction and add to your following.

Every November, writers around the world partake in National Novel Writing Month (NaNoWriMo) – a challenge in which participants have to write 50,000 words in 30 days. Hundreds of thousands of people get involved in this challenge and include #NaNoWriMo in their tweets to share their experiences and create a global support group.

As the hashtag is unlikely to be used by anyone else other

than National Novel Writing Month participants, I follow people who use it in their tweets using ManageFlitter Pro then tweet about my own #NaNoWriMo progress.

Soon after, I usually get an influx of writers checking out my profile and engaging with my tweets. As some of them won't be online right away, this method can actually lengthen the lifespan of a tweet. The attention continues as more people log into Twitter over the next few hours, sometimes for as much as a whole day!

RETWEETING PROMOTIONS

As a rule, I wouldn't recommend retweeting random artists who ask you to promote their work. If their work costs money, and if you don't want to be seen to endorse other people's products without being familiar with their work, it may breach the trust you've built up with your followers. If you know the artist and their work then that's different, but even then you should consider the potential effect it could have on your reputation.

What I do recommend is asking those random artists if they're giving away anything for free that you could promote. This is because, even if their work isn't any good, your followers won't feel cheated as they won't have spent any money. Operating in this way means that you're being both ethical to your followers and to the artists who sought help from you. It allows your reputation to benefit on both fronts and grow without spamming your followers with worthless promotions. By offering alternative support, you will benefit from reciprocal favours when you decide to do a free giveaway yourself.

Megastar indie author Hugh Howey attributes much of his

success to building up a bank of favours in this way. Cashing them in got him more exposure than he could manage getting himself by working alone.

ASKING FOR RETWEETS

I don't ask for retweets often, simply because I don't want to desensitise my followers. As a result, I can maximise the impact of my requests when I do ask. It's been proven that asking for retweets in the body of a tweet you want shared can result in more retweets. This can be done easily by adding "Please RT" at the end of the tweet you want promoted.

If you're planning to use this method when promoting an event or product, I would advise that you do so sparingly so you don't annoy your followers. Requesting retweets too often will only do you more harm than good in the long term, leading to unfollows and people skipping your tweets whenever they see them.

Aiming for quality over quantity can also help you when asking people for retweets. When I released my first book *The Winter Freak Show*, I tweeted a link and a request for retweets to two of my favourite bestselling authors – Anthony Horowitz and Darren Shan – explaining that their own books inspired my work. Both authors knew that I actively supported them on Twitter so it was clear that I wasn't faking admiration just to get retweeted.

Almost immediately, they both retweeted my tweet that announced my free giveaway and wished me luck. If you use this method when promoting your work, make sure you have a good relationship with whoever you want to retweet before you ask for their help. If you are truly a fan of theirs then promoting them beforehand shouldn't be a problem. There's no guarantee that they will reciprocate your support but it can't help to get in their good books before you ask for help. If they do retweet then be sure to thank them afterwards.

One day you might be asked to retweet someone because of your influential following. I've been in this position and I prioritise my most interactive followers over ones who have never tweeted me before asking me to promote them. It's helpful to remember that, just as much as you want your idols to like you, they want to stay in your good books to maintain your adoration. Showing them that you're a dedicated fan will make them want to keep you that way, so they'll often be happy to spend a few seconds promoting you to keep you happy.

RETWEETING CHECKLIST

In summary, when considering the topic of retweets, you should:

- o Practice retweeting to get used to it.
- o Ensure you are retweeting people and tweets that match your brand.
- o Experiment with the various ways you can retweet something.
- o Experience the pros and cons or retweeting tweets in different ways.
- o Try to get more credit for a retweet than the person who tweeted the original message by adding a comment.
- o Set rules for when and how often you are prepared to retweet other people's promotions.
- o Retweet selectively for maximum impact.
- o Build a good relationship with other Twitter users so you can ask for retweets without annoying them.
- o Aim to get retweets from powerful influencers.

DIRECT MESSAGING

Direct messages used to be limited to 140 characters (like tweets) but Twitter has expanded this limit to 10,000 characters. They are private and can only be shared between two accounts that follow each other. This means that you can have private conversations with your friends and followers, but you can't message anyone in this way if they don't follow you back. You can access your direct messages by finding them in the top panel on Twitter, next to the "Notifications" button.

When it comes to direct messages, many people feel strongly about how they should and – more importantly – should not be used. I've made mistakes in this area in the past.

Lucky, none of my followers berated me, possibly because many other users commit worse offences than my naïve misdemeanours.

I once sent personalised requests to garner some extra downloads during a free book giveaway. But never again. Of course, you can experiment and play around with direct messaging as much as you want. This section will simply offer you guidance based on what has worked well for me during my time on Twitter.

NEVER SEND AUTOMATED DMS

Many Twitter users choose to use free and paid applications to send automatic direct messages to everyone who follows them. This often comes as a note that reads something like this:

> Thanks for following me. Check out my stuff by following this link! LINK.EXAMPLE.COM sent by SpammerExample.com

It ends with a clickable link and the name of the app they used.

I get what these users are trying to do. People who use automated messages typically own accounts that are growing quickly, so they use template introductory messages to start conversations without having to message every new follower individually – a task that is virtually impossible to maintain if you get lots of followers every day. They're trying to show that they care but without spending too much time doing it. The result, however, causes more harm than good. Here's why:

1. The message isn't personalised, even if the

application includes the follower's name in a template message. The fact that the follower can actually see that the message was sent by an app (which is the app's way of advertising and getting revenue if it's free to download) exposes this off-putting truth, making it look like the sender sees their followers as numbers in a production line rather than real people.

2. Responding to direct messages takes time, and that's something everybody lacks. People who send these messages waste the time of their followers who have to trawl through their inbox for no reason.

3. Many people don't use direct messages because of the spam problem. If you're active and sociable on Twitter's main feed then people will interact with your tweets regardless of whether or not you send them direct messages. Messaging them directly as well just adds to their spam issues.

4. Many account holders with a large number of followers routinely ignore direct messages, preferring to spend their time on public tweets in which they are mentioned instead.

5. Beginning a relationship by trying to sell something often creates a bad first impression. Many people who respond to these messages only do so out of politeness.

A more respectful – and fruitful – approach would be to send a few genuinely personalised messages to a selection of new followers. This shows that you really care about some individuals and that you want to have a meaningful conversation. If this sounds like a waste of time, don't send any.

If you *are* going to send automated direct messages, then at the very least don't include a sales pitch. You might think that doing so will lead to extra sales for virtually no effort but I think that the best way to make long-term sales is to build up a relationship of trust with your followers through your public tweets. Treat them like your friends in real life, using the types of tweets we've already covered. Before you know it, your new followers will like and trust you, and begin to ask about your projects.

DMS FOR PRIVATE CONVERSATIONS

The whole point of direct messages is to have private conversations. It was only when companies got involved and saw their potential as a means of selling goods (or at least trying to) that direct messages became a cesspit of spam. If you consider yourself a creative person and not just a faceless entity then avoid ruining the experience for everyone.

If you want to use direct messages, then tweet the recipient and let them know that's what you're doing. They may be one of the people who ignore DMs and your message will be lost on them.

That doesn't mean you should ban talking about business altogether. Maintaining a business-like mind-set is essential for success. I definitely encourage using direct messages to conduct business, but only on a business-to-business level. I'm currently followed by J. K. Rowling's current agent. As an author, when this first happened, it was a "pinch me" moment. And what made it more astounding was that *he* instigated a direct message conversation with *me*! After seeing my tweets and follower interaction levels on Twitter, he invited me to send a copy of my latest manuscript to his company for his associates to consider. Sadly, this story doesn't have a fairy-tale ending. After reading the first few pages of one of my early manuscripts, his associate decided that it didn't appeal to them and politely rejected it – but my point still stands. J. K. Rowling's agent talked business with me, but we only did so because it was in the interest of both parties. Neither side felt like they were being sold something they didn't want. Always keep that in mind and it will put you in good stead when maintaining good Twitter etiquette.

Of course, you don't have to wait to be approached. Recently, I headhunted a graphic designer I wanted to work with after hearing that he had worked with an author whose book covers I thought were excellent. Having found the designer on Twitter, I followed him and sent him a tweet, explaining how I discovered him and suggested that I would be interested in working with him as long as the price was right. I introduced myself using a well thought-out, personalised message. A few hours later, he followed me back and asked me in a direct message to send him my email address so we could talk business.

Direct messages are better suited to collaboration than to selling as they allow you to talk about the nuts-and-bolts elements of your work without having to maintain your public persona of perfection. Plus, they enable you to share personal information without showing the rest of the world.

THE DELUGE OF SPAM

Whether you love to use direct messaging or not, you will almost inevitably find it to be a drain on your time as you grow your account.

The tactic for growth we will explore later in this book involves following many people over a long period of time, gradually pruning the people you follow in order to make you a powerhouse with an impressive following-to-follower ratio. Following lots of people who also follow you opens you up to receive a vast amount of direct messages.

As a result, I hardly ever use direct messages now simply because of the sheer amount of spam I get every day. I receive so many automated messages that it's impossible to keep up without giving up a significant chunk of time. Due to this deluge, I only ever look at my direct messages if someone asks me to so we can conduct business. Anything more than that is a waste of your time, which should be given sparingly so you have time to create new things as well as promote your existing creations. As a guideline, I would suggest focusing on the quality of your tweets to maintain your public presence, and use direct messages exclusively for collaborating as your account grows.

If everyone used direct messages in the way they were originally meant to be used – for private conversations – then using them would be a much more viable option. As I see it, however, they should be used only when necessary. And they should never be automated. That only wastes other people's time, and for that you will rarely be forgiven.

Direct Messaging Checklist

In summary, when thinking about direct messaging, you should:

- o Reply to a handful of relevant direct messages.
- o Learn the limits of direct messages.
- o Avoid common Twitter faux pas concerning direct messaging.
- o Introduce yourself in a direct message to someone who interests you.
- o Focus on using direct messages to build relationships rather than make quick sales.
- o Never use automated direct messages.
- o Personalize your messages to reap higher rewards.
- o Use direct messages primarily for behind-the-scenes business discussions and focus on using your tweets to talk to fans.
- o Prepare to change the way you use direct messages as your account grows.

HARNESSING THE POWER OF #HASHTAGS

Giving the hash symbol, #, a function other than using it to replace the word "number" originated on Twitter but has proven so successful that it has been adopted by Facebook and mainstream television networks, who use them to advertise their shows. The reason for this is that the humble hash symbol – when connected to the start of a word of short message – can be used effectively to group and organise opinions, regardless of speakers' geographical locations.

Hashtags are words or short messages that begin with a # symbol and are automatically hyperlinked. They can contain no spaces, and only letters or numbers, but no special characters or punctuation marks.

If multiple words are used in a hashtag, the first letter of each word is often capitalised to improve readability, sometimes it's easier for people to read when the whole hashtag is capitalised. This is purely cosmetic and they don't have to be entered exactly the same way when searching. Hashtags are not case sensitive.

By creating a hashtag, you can organise your tweets into specific feeds. For example, if you're working on three different projects at once but a follower is only interested in one of them then they can see updates about that particular project by clicking on its designated hashtag.

Similarly, by using other people's hashtags, you can reach a larger audience than you could by using your own, and possibly attract some of that audience to you. As a warning I must stress the importance of taking the time to understand other people's hashtags before contributing to them or hijacking them. People and companies have got into a lot of trouble for making the mistake of not researching a hashtag before they contributed, creating scenarios that have caused media outrage and even ended careers. It's best to do your homework first.

There are many types of hashtags, from personal ones used for organisations, to interactive public ones, to paid trending ones funded by companies.

All are available to be used by creative opportunists. Deciding which ones are appropriate is key to success, and that depends entirely on what you want to achieve. Below, I've noted a few important things to think about when constructing and searching for hashtags.

ORIGINAL HASHTAGS

By original hashtags I mean ones that you have invented that are unlikely to be used by other users. This section will talk about why it's good to use unusual hashtags in some cases. "Hang on! Didn't we just discuss how using popular ones can help you reach larger audiences and make your tweets more searchable?" Well, yes. Using common hashtags can certainly help with that. But using an original hashtag from time to time can benefit you in other ways.

Firstly, we have to remember that mastering Twitter is an art, and writing tweets the way Twitter expects is just one form of that art. As with other types of art, those who play with the form stand out from the crowd. On Twitter, this could entail using original hashtags as punchlines to jokes that feature in the main body of your tweets, or even as a second punchline to extend your joke. For example:

> At the supermarket a man threw some cheddar at me. I thought, "How dairy!" Sorry about the cheesy joke… #EnoughRoomToFetaHashtag

As you can see, the main body of the tweet sets up the joke and offers a punchline. Then the original hashtag adds another layer to the joke, making it funnier by fitting in as many cheese-based puns as possible. The separation of the hashtag from the main body of text supplies the reader with a natural pause that helps to maintain comedic timing, which is difficult to do on a screen and in just 140 characters.

You can use hashtags to connect your tweets about particular projects and make it easier for people to track updates on them. Using original hashtags in this way means that your tweets won't get lost in a river of unrelated messages as people can click on your chosen hashtag and see everything grouped conveniently together.

An added benefit is that your followers are more likely to stumble upon promotional links that could lead to sales as they won't have been drowned out by everyone else's tweets.

TRACKING HASHTAGS

You can track hashtags by locating them using Twitter's search bar or by clicking on them in the body of a tweet. Tracking a relevant hashtag is an easy way to encounter like-minded people.

This function can be useful to anyone on Twitter, regardless of their profession or interests. For creative professionals, they can be used to keep tabs on events, or track Q&A sessions.

Many celebrities use hashtags in this way. Barack Obama has used #AskObama to discuss policies with voters. People interested in the discussion could follow what other people had to say by clicking on the hashtag.

Disciplining yourself to use hashtags in your tweets can connect you with mentors and supporters who will offer you advice and encouragement. These people are more likely to read your tweets as they can relate to what you're trying to do.

Remember, great leaders are also great listeners. Growing your influence is just as much about following and listening to others as it is about broadcasting your own messages.

TRENDING HASHTAGS

Trending hashtags are important. Using them can help you reach massive audiences. It's like the difference between singing karaoke at your local bar, and being the support act for a world-famous rock star. Not everyone will be there to listen to you, but a few of the ones who aren't will take an interest anyway.

There are many methods for getting a hashtag trending nationally, or even globally. Some I can talk about in this chapter, while others are impossible to explain, being freaks of good fortune and public mood. Others still, are impossible to achieve, exclusively controlled by the Twitter A-listers, household names with millions of followers – that is, unless you become one of them.

PROMOTED HASHTAGS

One way to get a hashtag trending without mountains of luck, power, or Twitter know-how is to buy your place on the trending list with a promoted hashtag.

Twitter – just like Facebook – has set up online forms to help anyone part with their cash. Obviously, this isn't something most people can do as the move includes a hefty price tag – currently around $200,000 per day! The returns can be massive if done correctly, but I would argue that throwing money into Twitter advertising of this kind won't necessarily reap the rewards you hope to achieve. Many marketing campaigns are ignored because they seem contrived, or they are paid for by conglomerates that don't really get the essence of Twitter. Others garner an even worse fate, becoming hijacked by users who turn out-of-touch campaigns into global jokes. It's a dice-roll at best, and I wouldn't gamble with that kind of money.

Promoted hashtags work extremely well for TV networks promoting new shows that are launching the same day. Due to the nature of programmes airing live (even if they are prerecorded, they are happening now), they can become communal experiences. Seeing the hashtag trending on Twitter reminds potential viewers that the show is broadcasting that day and can even initiate some buzz before it starts.

The same tactic doesn't seem to transfer to book launches and gallery openings as they don't generally generate enough live mainstream interest to trend.

An example of a successful promoted hashtag came from the consumer goods giant Procter & Gamble. In 2015, they promoted #LikeAGirl – an interactive hashtag they used to get people involved in changing the negative connotations of doing something "like a girl." Due to its universal appeal and progressive attitude it did very well, inspiring debate and generating lots of buzz for the business. This process was helped along considerably by the company's TV ad that aired simultaneously during the Super Bowl commercial break. The right idea, combined with the right timing and exposure, can be extremely lucrative.

On the opposite end of the spectrum, McDonald's ran the hashtag #McDStories in 2012 and it was a dramatic failure. Instead of following the company's intention of sharing their best McDonald's stories, the public became inspired to contribute to the promoted hashtag with sarcasm. People tweeted things like:

> Dude, I used to work at McDonald's. The #McDStories
> I could tell would raise your hair.

> #McDStories I lost 50lbs in 6 months after I quit
> working and eating at McDonald's

Obviously, McDonald's didn't expect their hashtag to get hijacked. The mistake cost them hundreds of thousands of dollars in wasted advertising expenditure. Plus, there was the unquantifiable cost of the damage the campaign did to the business. I'm not telling you this to scare you, but to show you what could go wrong.

People, for better or worse, tend to get involved in hashtags that adhere to our familiar three golden rules of tweeting – offering inspiration, entertainment, or knowledge.

For artists, a promoted hashtag might be less likely to get hijacked than that of a large corporation. While a book launch might achieve the three golden rules, few authors can guarantee enough early readers to spark a worldwide debate, possibly because it takes longer than an hour-long TV slot to digest a full book. One author who could command the sort of surge necessary to trend globally is J K Rowling, and even her ability to do so diminished after launching the final Harry Potter novel.

HASHTAG GAMES

A better way to use the trending list to get people interested in you is to participate in hashtag games. These are hashtags that form part of a sentence or encourage creativity. They are usually open-ended so people can use their wit to take the hashtag in unexpected and hilarious directions. Some examples of past hashtag games include:

> #IfIHadAHoverBoardIWould
> #ExplainAFilmPlotBadly
> #MillennialResolutions

These games may seem trivial, but the truth is that humour often grows your Twitter following faster than anything else. Some of my most effective tweets have been contributions to hashtag games. When I contributed to #MillennialResolutions, I managed to produce the number one tweet on that hashtag in the world, gaining over 500 retweets and likes from one tweet.

Daniel Parsons
@dkparsonswriter

Learn how to even. #MillennialResolutions

RETWEETS 229   LIKES 296

8:08 PM - 30 Dec 2015

If you don't feel like you're a naturally funny person, don't worry. Hashtag games tend to inspire comedic responses and are invaluable for keeping your public image fresh and playful.

An added benefit to playing hashtag games is that they can help you extend your presence on Twitter without having to schedule tweets to be released throughout the night. If your contributions get retweeted enough to be put on the top feed for the hashtag then your exposure will last much longer than the usual 45-minute lifespan of an average tweet – sometimes by as much as two days.

My only issue with the top feed is that the tweets tend to be disproportionately representative of accounts with a high number of followers. The reason for this is that larger accounts' tweets get more initial exposure due to their existing followers. Therefore, they hit hashtags' top feeds more easily than smaller/newer users even when their tweets aren't as good. This may sound like the elite users have an unfair advantage, but that should motivate you. I've seen accounts with only a few hundred followers hit a trending hashtag's top feed. After that, Twitter's exposure takes over and the sky's the limit. Trending is possible. It just gets easier when you reach a few thousand followers.

A quick tip for getting ahead in hashtag games is to accompany your funny tweet with an image. This will make your tweet more noticeable. All you really need is enough interactions to get onto a hashtag's top feed. Hashtag games work like crowd pleasers; if they resonate with a hashtag's audience, they can help even the smallest voice be heard around the globe.

HASHTAG VOTING

Earlier, I mentioned complicit marketing – a process in which you allow readers to offer input into the construction of your current project, whether it's a book cover, music video, or an artistic choice. This is done by giving your followers options and asking them to vote on what they think will make it better. You remain in control, but you gain some valuable feedback before releasing your finished work.

Hashtags can be used to improve this process by also making your work more searchable. Before I explain all of the potential benefits of combining hashtags with voting, I'd like to share with you an example of how I've used them myself.

A while back I wrote a book called *Blott*. Its title referred to the hero of the story. When finalising my hero's name I decided to ask my followers' opinions to involve them in the decision. I gave them two options and asked them to consider which name would look better on the book's cover. The two hashtags I supplied were #Blott and #Blot. This experiment generated over 20 responses from a range of readers, with most of them including #Blott in their tweets, along with reasons for their decisions.

As well as gaining valuable feedback, having a whole tribe of people promoting your work and displaying a hashtag you designed has massive promotional benefits.

Hashtags trend when lots of people use the same one in their tweets in a short space of time – in most cases, a few thousand. It takes more than my 20 related tweets by 20 different people to get a hashtag trending but the required number is probably lower than you might think. I've seen hashtags trend with as few as 120 tweets. All it takes is a slow news day and the online world becomes open to opportunists, ready to fill the media void. That person could be you!

Also consider this: a famous business theory called the Rule of Seven states that people need to see a product seven times before they consider buying it. Since the rise of the internet, with its 24-hour-news-feed nature, I would argue that this number is double that in the digital age.

Generating a vote in the way I've described means that some people who follow your followers may see your work mentioned on their Twitter feed multiple times from several sources. This means that you can get people you don't know to recognise and become interested in your work simply through them seeing their friends talking about you in several places. Put simply, hashtag votes ensure that your work gets noticed by people who have never even heard of you, and you aren't bombarding them with advertising for it to happen.

GETTING A HASHTAG TO TREND

Hashtags trend on Twitter for various reasons. Some trends are initiated by celebrity scandals. Others are linked to political upheaval. And many start as simple word games that spread like proverbial wildfire. Massive events like the Olympics get people talking. And sometimes trending topics are started by something a pop star has done. Despite having to compete with all of these things, it's still possible to get a position in those coveted ten trending slots positioned next to Twitter's main feed. In fact, it might not be as difficult as you think, and here's why:

- Twitter's trending hashtags are personalised to each user, representing the most commonly occurring words used by the people they follow at any time. If you follow lots of accounts, then only hashtags that have thousands of contributors will tend to reach your top ten trending list. However, if you only follow a handful of accounts it may only require five or six related tweets to hit your trending list. Of course, the top slots are almost exclusively taken by major events, news, and viral games, but claiming them isn't impossible.

- Something you've said in the past may have trended on someone's Twitter feed without you even knowing about it. If you want to get into the upper echelons of trending hashtags, where thousands of people take notice of your work, you're going to need to be tactical about the kind of actions you take to maximise your tweets' exposure.

Below are the four best ways I have discovered for getting something trending on Twitter.

1. Paying to Promote a Hashtag

If you have enough money, you can pay Twitter $200,000 to put your hashtag at the top of the trending list. This is the only guaranteed way to get a trending hashtag, but it isn't always the best. This method works well for TV networks that want to create early buzz for a new show, but when businesses in other industries try to promote themselves in this way the result can often be underwhelming or – worse – counterproductive if the hashtag is hijacked by internet trolls.

Social media users like to feel like something became popular because they wanted it to, not because big businesses made it happen. TV shows thrive because of their communal, live nature which means that they're likely to trend even without a promotional boost as lots of users watch and discuss them when they are aired. Other products don't typically have this advantage.

2. Getting Your Followers to Vote

I've talked about this tactic in an earlier chapter but I want to stress its effectiveness. Complicit marketing engages your followers, making them feel just as much a part of the project as the original creator. By giving your followers two hashtag options, then asking them to choose their favourite and offer a reason for their choice, you inspire heated debate. As it's the internet, everyone likes to have their opinion heard. You can get a hashtag trending based on the relationships built up between you and the people who vote on your hashtag.

3. Coordinated Tweeting

If you don't have a large online following yet then you could try getting friends, family, and supporters to coordinate their tweets with you. This isn't generally the best method to take as friends and family are difficult to count on when it comes to actively participating in something that isn't necessarily important to them. Of course, this isn't their fault; people have busy lives and chose to prioritise things that matter to them personally so you shouldn't force them to get involved.

If you've only just started out on Twitter and have a small following, relying on personal contacts for help might be your best chance of getting a hashtag trending.

If you do have a large online influence then you can draw support from your existing followers. Many celebrities use this advantage when caught up in arguments with other A-listers. They will often form a hashtag to drum up extra awareness and get thousands of their fans to abuse their opponent. Now I'm not saying this behaviour is morally right but it does teach us a valuable lesson; if your hashtag involves a message that your followers can get behind passionately it has a much better chance of trending and boosting your personal brand.

4. THUNDERCLAP

Thunderclap is an online tool. It is designed to help you coordinate your tweets with others to get something trending on Twitter, Facebook, or Tumblr.

Scheduling tweets is not a new concept. People have been scheduling tweets in order to get their words in front of the most number of people for years. To a degree, Thunderclap also does this. What sets it apart from other apps is that it allows a crowd of people to schedule a template tweet all at the same time.

How it works is simple: a user sets up a campaign with a participant goal and a date by which those participants have to join. Then the user gets participants to sign up to the campaign up until the launch date. If the user reaches their goal then all of the participants will send out the same predetermined tweet, Facebook post, or Tumblr post at the same time and date, creating a barrage of synchronised media buzz for whatever the user wants to promote. If the campaign doesn't reach its participant goal then the synchronised tweet will never happen.

Using a tool like Thunderclap can be massively more successful and reliable than having to count on forgetful supporters to come through for you. It enables you to generate a coordinated flood of tweets by slowly growing participation numbers over a longer period of time. This decreases the element of luck that is usually involved in a coordinated social media campaign and ensures you a better chance of hitting that coveted trending hashtag list next to Twitter's main feed.

Think of it like a flash mob. If you walked to the middle of an airport and you started dancing, then asked friends and passers-by to get involved, how many would actually join in? Possibly a few spontaneous individuals might, but the turnout would be low and the quality of execution would lack the precision of a pre-planned routine. However, if you asked people over a long time period if they would like to join a flash mob, giving them instructions concerning the place and time and what dance moves to use, then the chances are higher that more people would turn up on the day, and those that did so would be better prepared. Thunderclap essentially turns a handful of freestylers into a flash mob that can cheer up the whole airport and maybe make the national news!

GAMING THE SYSTEM

When it comes to the internet, every major website on the planet, from Google to Amazon, is driven by big data, algorithms, and search engine optimisation.

If you know how the algorithms work for any particular website then you know how to beat their system and reach the most users. If you're on Amazon, that may mean selling a particular number of books within a particular timeframe to get into the charts. For Google, it may be using the correct words on your website so that your blog appears on Google's first page for certain search criteria. For Twitter, it's using hashtags, retweets, and follower growth to increase your influence.

Large websites keep their algorithms close to their chests. This is because they don't want people to game their system as it can degrade their website's ability to provide a good experience for its users.

One example of people gaming the system includes the simple information that you need 4,545 followers in order to follow more than 5,000 people on Twitter. That statistic was not released by Twitter. It was discovered by a user who split-tested lots of accounts, each with different levels of activity, to determine the numbers Twitter hides. That number changes as

Twitter alters its algorithms to keep people working cautiously rather than aggressively on growing a following, so that they don't ruin the user experience for everyone.

There is really only one way to game Twitter's system with hashtags and that's to include them in the name of your projects. This is a clever move that I first encountered when musician, music producer, and talent show judge Will.I.Am released his hit record #Power which trended on Twitter several times, bouncing back into the top ten trends multiple times. It did this is partly because both Will.I.Am and Justin Bieber – who was featured on the track – are major players on Twitter. Its unusual longevity on the trending list, though, is almost certainly due to its title starting with a hashtag. Every time someone tweeted about the song, they added the hashtag to the title, maintaining its trending status.

As you can probably tell, I liked this method so much I adopted it when naming this book. None of the other authors in my niche have chosen to tap into this extra promotional opportunity despite having Twitter followers who would be happy to help make their work go viral.

SUMMARY

So there you have it; several ways to get a hashtag trending. There are always ways to manipulate a system to your advantage – without breaking Twitter's rules. I need to emphasise that there is a difference between using a system, and abusing it. Abuse it at your peril – and expect to get your account shut down. Be creative and see what you can achieve with what you have learned. Just make sure that what you're doing won't ruin Twitter for others. In the words of Spiderman,

"With great power comes great responsibility." Use your power wisely.

Hashtags are at the heart of Twitter. Mastering these tips will enable you to organise your tweets, reach more people, and create media buzz around your newest creative project. Simple improvements could mean the difference between getting a handful of people talking about your work, and having it discussed by thousands.

HASHTAG CHECKLIST

In summary, you should:

- o Study trending hashtags and identify common themes.
- o Contribute to a trending hashtag.
- o Create an original hashtag of your own.
- o Attempt to make a hashtag trend.
- o Consider the costs, benefits, and risks of paying to promote a hashtag.
- o Join and try to win a hashtag game.
- o Create a poll using hashtags in your tweets.
- o Experiment with tools that help you make a hashtag trend.
- o Come up with a sharable hashtag for your artwork or product.

FOLLOWERS & FOLLOWING

Prominent business philosopher Jim Rohn once said, "You are the average of the five people you spend the most time with." By this, he suggests that everyone's mind-set is influenced by their peers; hanging around with lazy pessimists can make you one too, and spending time with motivated optimists can improve your own motivation. Likewise, you can fuel or drain those around you, depending on your own attitude.

While this quote might have been true years ago, the prevalence of social media in the modern world now means that its relevance has diminished. Nowadays you don't have to change your friends to succeed in life because the internet allows you to be influenced by positive figures even if you don't know them personally. Twitter has made the idea of limitless connections even more relevant due to its lack of barriers to celebrities and industry frontrunners, making inspirational figureheads more accessible than they have been at any point in history. At the click of a link you can see what the most productive members in any field are doing and model yourself on their actions. Some may even answer questions you send them.

Despite this new level of accessibility, what has become apparent is a tsunami of noise. Not only can you reach influencers but they can reach you... in their droves. Twitter's limitless friend expansion model has made it easy to find anyone on the planet but at the same time harder to block out unwanted voices and work out exactly who you should follow to improve the quality of your interactions. After all, knowing billionaires and moguls means nothing if they work in a completely unrelated field to you. An oil baron probably won't help you create a chart-topping album and a celebrity gardener won't know how to open doors for you as an art collector.

Having millions of followers means nothing if none of them interact with you. Many people have said this, but what they fail to mention is that interactive followers can be just as useless as silent ones if they aren't the right type of follower for you. This section will show you what to look for as a creative professional when following other users. The guidelines we explore will improve your follower growth, interactivity levels, and the quality of your interactions.

Who to Follow

When following other users, you have to think about what *you* look for when deciding whether to follow someone, and then make sure *you* display those same characteristics. You should never follow just anyone. This will help to you to get quality followers who are genuinely interested in the kind of content you produce.

I tend to follow writers, readers, librarians, literary agents, English teachers, booksellers, publishers, and similarly related accounts. That way I get to read tweets that interest me, and talk to people with similar interests.

ROLE MODELS

A good place to start is by following people who work in the same area of the arts as you do. They will give you ideas for the type of content you might want to produce. Not all of them have to follow you back. In fact, I would recommend initially following a few people that you know are never likely to follow you back but are key influencers in your field. Follow people who inspire you and whose tweets you actually want to read. Not only will they tweet things that you could retweet to your own followers, but they also make the whole Twitter experience more fun.

Consistency is the key to succeeding on Twitter, so following people who are already where you want to be will not only help you grow but will also motivate you to keep going. Following them first will make it a lot easier for you to fight through the slow initial stages of growth to a point where you start to see the real potential Twitter has to offer.

VERIFIED ACCOUNTS

I can't stress enough the importance of following some verified accounts, particularly if they're key players in your field. One benefit to being followed back by verified accounts is that they often don't follow many people so your account will stand out when other people are looking at who they deem important enough to follow.

Another reason to follow verified creative people is that they often work at the cutting edge of their industries so are a good benchmark for current working methods and the kind of work ethic you need for getting ahead of the pack.

Finally, being followed by them is taken seriously by the average person. It can make them take notice of you and grow your influence in the real world. I recommend focusing on following relevant verified users who work in your field, rather than just *any* verified user. If an unrelated verified account follows you first, however, which may become the case as your account grows, then I recommend always following them back, even if it's only for the prestige.

LANGUAGE

An account's primary language should be one of the first things you look at when thinking about following someone new.

As much as I would like to be able to speak every language in the world, I can only read English. As I can't understand other languages, I don't follow people who don't speak English.

The few exceptions to this idea include accounts that show that they understand English by occasionally retweeting English messages, and relevant verified accounts. Following them back won't make their tweets easier to understand, but it might keep them from losing interest in your tweets and unfollowing you.

Remember, you're looking for people who can help you build a relevant audience for your work. Understanding each other is essential for this process.

ACTIVITY

Many Twitter users follow other people in the hope that they'll reciprocate sometime in the next few days. Officially, an inactive user has an account that hasn't tweeted anything for a month. I consider accounts inactive well before this point – usually if they haven't tweeted anything within the past two weeks. If you want other users to follow you back when you follow them – which is one of the most practical growth methods on Twitter – then only following people that have tweeted in the past fortnight ensures a greater chance of success.

Users that haven't tweeted in that time possibly haven't been on Twitter for two weeks and are unlikely to return soon, if at all. Following them will be a largely pointless activity. Not only will they not follow back but they also won't tweet anything interesting or interact with your tweets.

Following lots of inactive Twitter users is an inefficient way to grow so you should try to only follow active accounts. The more recently and frequently a person has tweeted, the better.

How to Follow & Unfollow

We must discuss how to make the process of following people a safe one. Unfollowing accounts may be a little more precarious than you realise, and we'll discuss it in detail shortly.

Following to Be Followed

One of the fastest ways to grow on Twitter is to follow people who interest you and hope that they follow back. If they prove to be inactive or don't tweet anything of interest, then unfollowing them will enable you to maintain a good following-to-follower ratio and allow you to follow other people in the future. (See more on this in the section entitled *Following-To-Follower Ratio*.)

Following Limits

Twitter imposes limits on the amount of people you can follow in any 24-hour period. These limits aren't fixed and depend entirely on the size, influence, and activity of your account.

Twitter doesn't release their exact guidelines to stop spammers from taking advantage of the knowledge. The only limit they *do* disclose is that no account, regardless of its size, can follow more than 1,000 people in a day. You shouldn't need to worry about hitting this limit for a while as only accounts with over 10,000 followers can follow hundreds of people at once without getting suspended. And even then, I would proceed with caution due to Twitter's tendency to change its limits and keep users guessing.

If you have a new account with no followers, the rule of thumb is to start by following a small number of relevant accounts – possibly 20 per day. When you hit 100 followers, you can increase it to 25. Then at 400 followers, you can jump to following 40 per day, and so on. Once you hit 1,000 followers, you can follow around 90 accounts every day, incrementally increasing this number until you hit 10,000 followers. At that point you should be able to follow 500 people each day without risking suspension. Although reports say you can follow 1,000 accounts at once when you exceed 10,000 followers, I would never risk being at the top of the limit, even with 90,000 followers. Not only is it safer but, while you're doing this, you will attract organic followers that you may want to follow back. If you've already used up your follows for the day, you won't be able to do that.

You aren't monitored on the specific number of people you follow every day, but you are on the number of people you follow in relation to the amount of followers you have. It's all relative. An account that has 20,000 followers can follow 500 people in one sitting because that only makes up 2.5% of their following. But if a new account with 200 followers tried the same thing, that would equate to 250% of their followers – a rate of expansion that Twitter associates with spammers.

You should also consider how many tweets and direct messages you send because Twitter also interprets people who tweet or direct message their followers hundreds of times a day as potential spammers. This makes sense as nobody is so exciting that they need to tweet 300 times in a day, and nobody has enough time to contribute to 300 conversations. If you do this, not only are you not spending enough time on your creative work, but it could lead to your account being suspended.

Likewise, if all of your tweets include links then there's a high likelihood that you're displaying spammer-like activity and risk suspension. So much of mastering Twitter is knowing your boundaries and not being annoying. If you can make the whole thing enjoyable and act like a real person then this shouldn't be an issue.

FINDING PEOPLE TO FOLLOW

If you're wondering where you find and follow people who might be interested in your account then you're not alone. Every once in a while, users tweet me to ask how I found them.

One method is by searching keywords and hashtags in Twitter's search bar. By filtering it to show *accounts* as opposed to *tweets* you will often find other creative professionals or industry experts in your field with relevant bios and similar interests.

For example, searching for *author* or *literary agent* presents writers with an almost endless list of potential networking contacts. You can then follow any who seem to be likely contenders for following you back, and disregard those who don't interest you.

Another way to find potential followers is to look at the followers lists of others in your field. You'll get the best results by searching lists of those who have a fairly balanced following-to-follower ratio but who are at a more advanced stage than you. I find this method works better for selecting suitable followers than using Twitter's search bar as people following the sort of person you want to become will also be likely to take an interest in me. My only caveat here is to make sure your model user is growing by more followers than you follow each day. This stops you from overlapping your previous efforts and repeat-following the same users, which we know is bad practice. To do this effectively you need to:

- Ensure you have a well-crafted bio and tweets that are relevant to your followers, offering the three key principles of Twitter: entertainment, inspiration, and knowledge.

- Tweet mainly in the language in which your work is produced. That's how you'll reach your primary audience.
- Be active and accessible, following different people each day so that you don't get a bad reputation for repeat-following.
- Keep a good ratio to help prune the dead wood from your following list to maintain growth, but don't do it too much so you remain approachable.
- Become verified if you think you're eligible. But don't worry if you're not verified as it won't limit your growth.

Doing all of these things will make you the ideal person to follow.

FOLLOWER LISTS

Creating lists on Twitter is useful as it enables you to separate your high-priority followers into categories. A list's purpose is to filter tweets that you see on your main feed so that you only see the tweets of people included on that list. This is an effective way to see and interact with your priority followers as they would usually get drowned out by the white noise of your main feed amidst the other people you follow. You can use this method to show them that you care about what they have to say outside of what they say directly to you. In short, it enhances the quality of your discussions with the people who are most likely to be interested in your creative work.

Writers might start by creating lists for readers, writers, publishers, agents, and so on. Or they could just have one list called "book lovers" which would cover all bases. It depends how many people they want to include in that list and how much attention they plan to show individuals. Other artists can use equivalent labels to categorise their followers. For example, a musician could create lists for producers, DJs, singers, agents, and publicists.

Just don't name your lists "Priority Followers" or something to that effect as the names of your lists are public by default. People know when they have been added to one. While that might flatter those included it could also make them feel like the targets of a marketing ploy. And people who notice that they're *not* included might be insulted and stop talking to you because they think you don't consider them to be a priority. Naming your list(s) appropriately can make all the difference. Remember to be strategic when categorising people into lists.

THE DANGER OF REPEAT-FOLLOWING

With over 300 million active monthly users, it may seem like you'll never encounter the same user twice, but when you've been on the site for a while and have followed thousands of accounts, you will discover just how incestuous some communities can be. If you're not careful, you can mistakenly follow the same people repeatedly. That's a tabooed practice that can make you more enemies than allies.

People hate being constantly followed and unfollowed by the same person. It's annoying and makes it seem as though you're just a number and that the person churning followers isn't even reading your biography. When you first join Twitter and only follow a handful of people, avoiding following the same people multiple times is easy, but as you grow, remembering who you've followed in the past can get difficult. There is a worthwhile application I will recommend to help alleviate this issue later in more detail, (see Twitter Tools for details).

The dangers of repeatedly following someone can be lethal. It can result in Twitter's systems flagging you as a spammer, getting you reported by other disgruntled users, or your account being suspended. It's possible to ask Twitter for the suspension to be lifted after your first offence but this is a risky way to conduct business. One false slip could lead to you losing your account altogether, along with hours of work, forcing you to start over from scratch. If someone hasn't followed you back in the past then following them again will only cause irritation, for them and for you.

AGGRESSIVE FOLLOWER CHURN

Follower churn is the process by which an account follows lots of Twitter users – sometimes hundreds of new users every day – and then unfollows the ones that don't follow them back to free up space so that they can follow more. As this method was originally adopted by spammers who were oblivious to the interests of the people they followed, it got a bad name. The spammer approach was labelled "aggressive follower churn" due to its focus on extreme growth, regardless of the people involved. These spam accounts typically tweet constant links to products and services that may not even interest their followers. As a result, aggressive follow churn is outlawed by Twitter. It can lead to an account being suspended because it can ruin the user experience for everyone.

Now this may sound like an unethical way to grow but creative professionals can learn a lot from the process. It doesn't rely on luck, is completely free, and almost guarantees growth. And what's more, it *can* be done in a moral way.

My own account's growth implements similar principles, but applied ethically. Instead of indiscriminately following anyone, I only follow those who are likely to take a genuine interest in my tweets, or who interest me. Learning how to do this with laser precision will lead to more followers *and* quality interactions from your audience. If done correctly, it won't ruin the Twitter experience; it will enrich it for everyone.

YOUR FOLLOWING-TO-FOLLOWER RATIO

Following and interacting with celebrities is thrilling. It makes you feel like a peer, gaining an insight into the lives of people you respect. I follow a handful of my favourite celebrities because they inspire, entertain, and teach me, but I don't follow too many for one simple reason: they rarely follow back. You'll quickly find that most celebrities tend to be followed by many more people than they follow.

If your intention is to grow your Twitter account then following lots of celebrities isn't the way to go. When checking out a potential follower's content, language, and activity you should make sure that their following-to-follower ratio isn't stacked against you.

If a person has 4 million followers and only follows 200 people then they're highly unlikely to follow you back. Targeting accounts that follow more than half the number of people that follow them is a sound strategy as probability suggests that they are 50% likely to follow you back. Although the true follow-back rate will probably be closer to 20%, that still offers you a worthwhile return over time. I occasionally stretch this guideline to follow verified or celebrity accounts with a reasonable ratio as the kudos of being followed by famous people is worth the extra risk.

Generally, the key is to use your own judgment as you grow more powerful and learn what parameters work well for achieving your goals.

GETTING A GOOD RATIO

When it comes to your own following-to-follower ratio, you will initially follow lots of people but lack followers. Over time I would recommend pruning who you follow, cutting your ties with unresponsive or inactive contacts to achieve this. If nothing else, it allows you to surpass the glass ceiling that only allows you to follow 5,000 users without having more than 4,545 followers. As your following grows and your own ratio improves, you'll start getting follow backs from more challenging targets who will be attracted by the powerful platform you've built for yourself.

Just don't go overboard with the pruning. Firstly, having a

ratio that's too impressive will put off potential contacts who may be active and engaging but won't follow you organically because they might think that there's no chance you will ever follow them back.

Secondly, cutting lots of active contacts will lead to you being unfollowed *en masse*. A smart move for maximising sustainable growth is to maintain a good ratio, but not go overboard, at least not until you become a household name and can get away with it.

The average person defines success on Twitter as having lots of followers while only following a handful of people back. However, that's like saying a company is successful because it has lots of employees even if it makes no profit. What most people don't realise is that having lots of followers while only following a handful back doesn't actually mean you're influential. Yes, you'll look powerful, but true power on Twitter is linked to the level of engagement your tweets attract. So, following lots of people back might not look impressive, but it generates real power. Below I will explain why having a good – but not amazing – ratio is better for most creative professionals.

As the number of your Twitter followers grows, you will also usually notice that the number of people you follow grows too. While some people see this as cheating, I wouldn't say so. Celebrities often follow only a few close friends, while they may have millions of followers themselves. Users who have grown their followers by following lots of people are often considered to have cheated the system. People who hold that opinion often don't see the benefits of the two-way links that are created by growing in this way.

Following crowds of people means that you're able to

direct message them – the possible benefits of which were described earlier (when done carefully and ethically). Showing that you follow a portion of your followers back and reply to most comments – unlike lots of celebrities – can also make you more attractive to follow as it shows the average person that you're down-to-earth and won't ignore them if they follow you or tweet you messages. In turn, that makes your followers more likely to comment on your tweets, which acts as a beacon for interested strangers who may then see you as the central figure of a creative network in your field.

Following more people than a conventional "celebrity" may make you look less influential even if you both have the same number of followers. It suggests that you have to follow people just to get followers yourself. I think that some figures that combat that assumption might surprise you.

When I compared my account (which follows back thousands of active, relevant people who interest me) with genuine celebrities who have a similar number of followers but only follow a handful of other verified accounts, what I discovered was that the level of interactions our tweets received were surprisingly similar. Of course, some celebrities get higher engagement due to having abnormally active fans, but many actually get fewer interactions per follower than I do. Twitter doesn't just benefit traditional celebrities. You can gain just as much influence as them, if not more, by reciprocating follows and being approachable.

Having said that, I'd still encourage you to prune the number of people you follow occasionally because having a positive ratio demonstrates that you care about the quality of people you follow and that you don't just follow anyone. A positive ratio makes you look like an authority in your field, providing social proof for potential collaborators and business contacts.

There are several ways to get a good ratio without losing influence. One is by not following *everybody* who follows you. Over time, this ratio will form a widening gap that works in your favour. Alternatively, you could use Twitter apps to reveal accounts that are no longer active or that have terrible ratios. (See Twitter Tools for details.) The reason I brought up that second characteristic is because account holders that follow hundreds of users, but only have a few followers, are the complete opposite of an A-lister. Their bad ratio means that they don't manage their accounts well so aren't likely to see many of your tweets and won't notice or care if you unfollow them. They sometimes even turn out to be fake followers that were originally mistaken for real people and got followed.

Just be careful when pruning the number of people you follow. Cutting away the wrong accounts can seriously damage your reputation and influence on Twitter, whereas cutting the right ones can help you grow and thrive.

WHO NOT TO FOLLOW

Twitter is a minefield when it comes to following people. If you don't know what to look out for then you can soon find yourself surrounded by accounts that tweet meaningless drivel, unwanted profanity, shameless self-promotion, and harmful abuse, and offer no enjoyment whatsoever to your Twitter experience.

After using the site for four years, I've developed a keen eye for pinpointing accounts that are detrimental to growth and the quality of my interactions. In this section we will move through the safari park of unsavoury animals you can find roaming the plains of Twitter. Some are dangerous predators and others massive herbivores, but all should be treated with caution. We will begin with the more obvious beasts and then uncover the masters of camouflage.

I would discourage automatically following back people who follow you but crucially don't fit into the guidelines explored in the previous chapter. If you begin to follow people that have irrelevant content, don't speak your language, and hardly ever tweet, then your growth will slow as you won't be reaching your true audience. To make matters worse, you will come up on several lists throughout Twitter that are targeted by spammers who will follow you simply because they think that you always follow back. Every time you follow these accounts, you become more detached from your target audience and attract more undesirable followers. In short, try to remain focused on following only people who are relevant to your success. Remember, quality, not quantity.

SYMBOL ACCOUNTS

Accounts whose names consist of symbols and whose profile images often feature teens smoking or something to that effect, tend to be pointless identities whose sole mission is to collect followers. They will often tweet about following back and creating "follow trains" to grow that number.

The purpose of these Twitter accounts is a mystery as they don't provide good content or try to sell anything. If you choose to play their game and exchange follows with them, you will soon find your follower base overcome with irrelevant figures who only follow you so that you will follow them in return. Steer clear.

PICTURE ACCOUNTS

These are similar to symbol accounts but they occasionally provide entertainment – mostly in the form of images. While some are benign and family-friendly, tweeting images of baby animals and sunsets, others are more sinister, churning out pornography and clickbait news stories. If there's a particular picture account that you want to follow as it feeds into your area of expertise then by all means follow it, but bear in mind that it will probably attract more accounts that may be less relevant.

Picture accounts, like symbol accounts, often move in packs. Following one will more than likely attract others over the coming days – many with less than savoury subject matter. These types of accounts can spread through Twitter like an infection if allowed to, leveraging their impressive follower numbers and the amount of lists they appear on to grow rapidly.

SPAM ACCOUNTS

Spam accounts endlessly try to flog stuff. There are two types; ones that share the same growth method as picture and symbol accounts, and ones that would not meet your normal following criteria. Neither have a good reputation.

There are large-scale spammers, the type that are usually run by companies that grow quickly using automated processes. When these accounts reach mammoth sizes, they use the platform they have created for themselves to spew a constant river of links to things they are trying to sell. In some of the most persistent cases, they can broadcast hundreds of automated tweets every day, targeting every person that follows them with no consideration for their demographics or interests. Large-scale spammers can be extremely annoying and are the reason why Twitter enforces their growth-limiting and account-suspending procedures.

Then there are the misunderstood spammers – a category that many creative professionals, particularly writers, fall into when they don't "get" Twitter. Believing that it's purely a way to sell stuff, they tweet nothing but endless sales pitches to every new follower, asking them to buy their work, or like their Facebook page (possibly because they prefer Facebook to Twitter). These people often wonder why their account gets ignored and, as a result of this lack of interaction, quickly lose interest in social media. It's because they don't understand how or why they should build relationships with their fans before asking for the sale.

Don't follow either type of account – this will benefit you as they won't be interested in what you have to say as much as you aren't interested in them. Only quick sales matter to spammers. They don't use the power of loyal followers.

CHRONIC UNFOLLOWERS

Certain Twitter users fake success by growing in the normal way – producing great content and following lots of people – and then later unfollow almost everyone in one mighty swoop, only to start again. I call these people chronic unfollowers. What they are doing is giving themselves an impressive following-to-follower ratio to make them appear to have genuine influence. To this, I guess you might say, "So, fake it 'til you make it? That's a good plan, right?" Wrong.

Chronic unfollowers rely on people not noticing their tactics. What cripples them is that their most interactive followers *will* often notice their insult and unfollow them in return. The people who keep following them will typically be inactive or spammy users. As a result, the practice leads chronic unfollowers to grow more slowly than other accounts, being burdened by a large proportion of inactive followers who never share their content or interact with their tweets.

The way to deal with chronic unfollowers is to simply not follow them back, or if you spot the signs, don't follow them in the first place.

TROLLS

Online trolls frequently appear in mainstream headlines for threatening celebrities or bullying innocent people. They are individuals who take it upon themselves to harass and make fun of other people on social media, hiding behind the anonymity that the internet provides. Luckily, I haven't encountered this spiteful breed on Twitter yet. The worst abuse I get tends to take the form of sarcastic witticisms, but I know that even those comments are normally written with humorous intentions, so I wouldn't consider myself a victim. Not everybody is so lucky.

Obviously the problem with internet trolls is that it's impossible to predict who might be one. As you grow and expose yourself to an increasingly large audience you become more at risk of becoming a victim of trolls. They seem to gravitate to successful people because they are the most accessible targets, seemingly motivated by jealousy. Luckily, there are several ways to avoid falling victim.

You can start by being nice to everyone. Even if someone says something that might be offensive, always assume it's a joke that got lost in translation. That way you will feel better and react in a more professional manner.

A second way to avoid trolls is not to tweet about controversial subjects. I never discuss religion, politics, social issues, or any other topics that might make me a target of hate. I suggest that you adopt this tactic as a general rule on Twitter if you want to maximise your growth. Discussing controversial topics will divide your followers based on strong opinions, possibly causing some of them to unfollow or oppose you.

Of course, if you do find yourself being attacked by a persistent troll, you can always instruct Twitter to block them from seeing your content. Those users will be able to create new accounts just to confront you but blocking them should be enough to stop their attacks.

FAKE FOLLOWERS

Fake followers are accounts that click farms (sweatshop-like companies whose employees control thousands of accounts) use to follow paying clients *en masse*. They rarely tweet and don't represent a real human, although they try to impersonate them. As a way of protecting their fake accounts, the companies that run them will often instruct them to follow people who have not paid for their services. The reasoning behind this is that thousands of fake followers that all follow the same people on the same day can be seen as suspicious by Twitter's policing algorithms. As a result, fake accounts that get caught are suspended. Having all of their fake accounts deleted by Twitter in bulk is detrimental to the business model of click farms. Not only will they have to create new accounts, which wastes time and money, but they will also have to deal with customers who have previously bought fake followers but suddenly lost them overnight and are now unhappy. Arranging for their fake accounts to follow people who haven't paid for their services occasionally makes click farms' accounts' activities less coordinated and harder to track and identify.

Fake followers can be difficult to identify as they are designed to look and act like real people, albeit largely inactive ones. They typically pose as pretty, young women and have a philosophical or funny quote as their bio. Usually, the first few that follow you will slip under your radar and get followed back. However, as more become attracted to your account, you will notice multiple followers that share the same profile picture or bio description, or, in some cases, both.

Another giveaway of this type of account is that their handle will be @Jenny183623947, or @fg65726cn89. Few real people would choose this type of handle. They will also have lots of their followers with a similar format of handle. That's because they were computer-generated.

The reason fake followers are sometimes hard to identify is because their creators are adapting, looking for new ways to appear human and not get culled by Twitter. Sometimes they appear as people other than young women, but that seems to be the standard disguise at the moment.

To those who are used to internet spam, these accounts stand out right away. If you're a less experienced social media user, they will be convincing enough to follow. Even now I don't always see through their masks. When you know what to look for they become more obvious and easier to avoid.

THE DANGER OF BUYING FAKE FOLLOWERS

There is a shortcut to getting a huge number of followers. That option is to purchase fake followers from people who sell them. Doing so is supposed to make users who want to attract genuine followers look popular so that they grow faster. You can buy different amounts of followers, ranging from 100 to 100,000+, depending on your budget.

As tempting as these services may sound, the truth is that buying fake followers can do you more harm than good. If you're tempted to try them, don't do it. Ever. Buying followers has dire implications, and certainly won't achieve your primary goal of getting interactions.

You can identify people selling fake followers a mile away. They claim to be able to provide you with thousands of "genuine" (ha!) Twitter followers, Facebook Likes, or YouTube views for a few dollars or pounds. This deal may seem like a massive time-saver for busy people, but the reality is that these followers are fake accounts. And that's the best case scenario. The worst is being sent nothing and having your bank account details stolen!

At one point, sellers used to describe their deals in their bios. It was only when Twitter became more advanced and put systems in place that scoured bios for spammy terms that they were forced to become smarter.

Now they have humanised their bios, professing to enjoy long walks and rock music, and have profile pictures of real human beings. Don't be fooled by this charade. Their background image will display their price-list in a way that's hard for Twitter's spam-hunting software to detect. These aren't real accounts. They are just as fake as the followers they sell and should be avoided.

Having these fake followers can stunt your influence. And this is true now more than ever.

Firstly, what you have to consider is that none of these fake followers offer meaningful interaction. Once they have followed you, they will be dormant.

Secondly, you have to consider the future. Look at Facebook and how their model for business pages has evolved. Once, when you sent out a Facebook post, everyone who liked your page would see it. Now, in an attempt to heighten profits, Facebook has changed so only 2-18% of the people who liked your page see any individual post. To reach the rest, your post has to have a high interaction level with that sample group, or you have to pay to "boost" the post.

The people who once bought fake Facebook likes now often find themselves broadcasting posts to the fake portion of their followers and are never able to reach their real supporters because those fake followers don't provide the early interaction their posts require. In short, the Facebook pages have become pretty much useless in many cases. This has happened to thousands of people and teaches the lesson that, on social media, engagement takes priority over follower numbers. Cutting corners doesn't pay.

Twitter has already introduced an algorithmic system in recent months that limits the exposure of tweets with low levels of interaction. If Twitter decides to go even further and adopt the same model as Facebook over time then having fake followers will inhibit the effectiveness of every tweet you send, massively reducing connection with your real audience.

There is the real possibility that you could see your account suspended if Twitter's algorithms think that you've bought fake followers and flag up your growth as suspicious.

Needless to say, I disapprove of buying fake followers. They are useless and a time bomb waiting to destroy your account.

FOLLOWING & FOLLOWERS CHECKLIST

In summary, you should:

o   Follow people who share your artistic interests.
o   Follow people who interest you if you're a new Twitter user, regardless of whether or not they are likely to follow you back.
o   Come up with your ideal follower and look for people with those same qualities.
o   Start by following more people than follow you.
o   Follow lots of people.
o   Don't worry about your following-to-follower ratio until you have a few thousand followers.
o   Occasionally prune the people you follow to achieve a good following-to-follower ratio by cutting out accounts that are inactive or irrelevant.
o   Always follow back verified accounts that follow you.
o   Consider using Twitter's lists function to organise people into categories.
o   Think outside the box when searching for people to follow.
o   Follow people back if you think they could help your career, even indirectly.
o   Don't follow back undesirable accounts.
o   Avoid any follow activity that could damage your account's long-term success.
o   Ignore or block internet trolls.
o   Avoid aggressive follower churn by growing purposefully but ethically.
o   Discourage the success of the fake follower business model.

MAKING MONEY ON TWITTER

So far we've looked into how to gain influence on Twitter and use it to gather a following of avid supporters. However, we are yet to discuss how to monetise that following.

Twitter isn't the best way to sell stuff directly – particularly if the unit cost of whatever you want to sell is low. If you're an artist selling individual paintings for hundreds of pounds, you might see a benefit in direct-selling Twitter ads, but for writers and musicians who sell products that only cost a few pounds, the cost of an ad often outweighs the revenue generated by sales.

But that doesn't mean you can't use Twitter to make money if you're a writer or musician. You just have to avoid selling directly and go about it in a different way.

As I've mentioned previously, you won't get far on Twitter if you only ever tweet messages asking your followers to buy your merchandise. To sell in volume, you will almost certainly have to pay for adverts. And that is something you shouldn't go into without some prior knowledge otherwise it will result in losing money.

This section will explore how to run Twitter ads successfully, including the pros and cons involved and how they can be used to great effect.

Types of Twitter Ads

I have serious reservations when it comes to spending ludicrous amounts of money on Twitter ads when they are likely to yield a loss if you don't know what you're doing.

Setting up an ad is a simple but specific process. As a result, Twitter makes it very easy to spend a lot of money on their platform. If you're going to try your hand at advertising here, make sure you have enough money to sustain yourself.

Lately, it's been widely documented that Facebook ads are proving to be highly profitable for those who know how to use them. Many creative professionals have notably made a small fortune using Facebook ads and have begun to develop similar strategies for Twitter.

I recently took a course on the subject run by a bestselling author who used online ads to make his fortune and, while I would argue that there is no guarantee that you will be successful as many different factors determine the profitability of an ad campaign, I have seen that it's possible to make money in this way. You just have to optimise your ads through trial and error, monitoring their performance as you change their image and text over time.

If you want to experiment with this then you'll have to know some context on the subject. Firstly, it's important to know that there are many different types of Twitter ads and that all of them have varying degrees of success depending on your goal. You can pay to promote:

- Your account.
- A single tweet.
- An innovative lead generation option called a Twitter Card.

136

All of these can benefit you in some way but not all of them will make you money. I'll show you a brief breakdown of how they work but for more information I would highly recommend doing some extra research around this topic or possibly even joining a course that could help you bypass an expensive learning curve.

PROMOTING YOUR ACCOUNT

Paying to promote your account positions it near the top of users' feeds and follow lists. The goal of this type of campaign is to get more followers by exposing you to more people. Twitter only charges you for an ad that gets an interaction – a deal that may seem like a bargain to the untrained eye – but what that actually means is that you get charged every time someone clicks on your profile.

Twitter charges premium prices for this privilege as they believe it to be a superior deal to traditional media outlets that charge a fixed price for ads, regardless of whether anyone responds to them.

I would suggest that promoting your account isn't worth the expense as you should be able to grow your followers by following the free and cheap growth methods discussed in this book. Admittedly, my methods are a little more labour intensive but they work efficiently and can lead to you getting active followers faster than most people's budgets could handle if they paid to do the same thing.

PROMOTING A TWEET

You might consider promoting a tweet if you want to build your followers or interactions, or if you're advertising something and want to send people to a sales page.

Promoting a single tweet works in a similar way to promoting your account, but instead of placing your profile at the top of people's follow list, it positions a tweet you write in a premium position in people's feeds so that more people see it. Using this method means that you get charged any time someone follows you, but also any time someone clicks on your tweet or any links or images attached to it. As a result, I would suggest that this sort of advertising isn't worthwhile for most people who just want to grow their presence on Twitter.

It can be useful if you sell items with a high ticket price. Say, for example, you're a sculptor who sells pieces of art for several hundred pounds and you want to send fans to a sales page, this method works well. Likewise, creators who run premium online courses can benefit greatly from promoted tweets. The highly profitable products you're selling make enough profit to cover the costs of the promotion. For authors and musicians who don't make as much money per sale, the conversion rate would almost certainly be too low to make this method worthwhile. In those cases, making a profit is possible but challenging.

TWITTER CARDS

Offering Twitter Cards is a relatively new development on the platform. This method is effective for those who want to build a mailing list. It works by presenting users with a free product that might interest them. Instead of asking them to part with cash, you asks for information – namely their email address. This signs them up to your mailing list without having to leave Twitter and go to another website.

As you won't make any money immediately, this idea may seem terrible. However, information is more valuable than quick sales, particularly if you want to build a long-term, loyal fan base of paying supporters. Selling products gives you short-term success, but building a mailing list is like buying regular customers, and the fastest way to build one is to give something away for free. This could be an ebook or an exclusive song. It develops a growing list of loyal supporters who will pay for your art, now and in the future. Once you've paid once, you have access to those people forever.

For writers in particular – and I don't see why it couldn't also work for musicians and artists – a mailing list is widely considered the best way to sell products. In comparison to social media sites, where adverts are fleeting and can easily be missed, emails last until they are manually deleted which means they are much harder to ignore.

By giving you their details via Twitter Cards, people who receive your emails are actively telling you that they want to receive news about your work. They're your priority tribe who buy into your brand and are most likely to interact favourably with new products you launch in the future. If you don't mind writing emails to those fans, you can offer them exclusive deals whenever you launch a new product, using their enthusiasm as a springboard to launch new products and generate early buzz. As your mailing list grows, the boost created in this way will provide enough publicity to attract fresh fans who wouldn't even know about your work if not for the buzz generated by your high priority tribe.

BIDDING

Twitter ads work on a bidding system where you have to state the ideal price you would like to pay for an interaction on your ad. People or companies that bid higher will get their ad distributed faster and reach more people in a shorter period of time. As a result, Twitter encourages people to bid more for their adverts, pushing up the price people are willing to pay by suggesting that their audience will be small or non-existent if they bid low. The reality, however, is that Twitter will still distribute a seller's ad even if they've bid a low amount. The ad will just be displayed to fewer people per day as sellers that bid higher will be given priority service.

The cost of an ad can be driven down to be affordable as long as you don't mind progressing more slowly. For those who plan long term, this approach shouldn't be a problem.

As a writer or musician, you could use this method with Twitter Cards to get people onto your mailing list. As long as you're certain you can make a profit on each subscriber on your list, your aim of making money from your art is still possible in the long term.

The benefit of having a growing mailing list is that each time you launch something new you will typically be able to reach more fans and make more money during the event. This, in turn, will help grow your reputation with potential fans outside of your list who are more likely to encounter your art organically.

CONCLUSION

As a creative professional, building trust is the only way to establish and grow a long-term brand. Twitter isn't a get-rich-quick scheme. It can help you expand your income but, as an artists, it takes a while to grow a trusting relationship with your supporters. Quick sales are fast and can plummet at a moment's notice, but a loyal audience can generate a stable income for the rest of your life.

MAKING MONEY ON TWITTER CHECKLIST

In summary, to monetise Twitter, you should:

- o Avoid tweeting "buy my stuff." It doesn't work.
- o Tweet content that entertains, inspires, and provides knowledge to gain your followers' trust.
- o Understand the difference between promoting your account and a single tweet.
- o Favour promoting your tweets over your account.
- o Set up a website that can collect your potential fans' email addresses.
- o Use Twitter Cards to build a mailing list.
- o Use that mailing list to make your advertising profitable if your art has a low unit cost.
- o Minimise your costs by being smart with Twitter's bidding system.
- o Drive down the cost of your ads over time.
- o Use trial and error to optimise the effectiveness of your Twitter ads.
- o Maintain your focus on long-term growth over quick sales.

TWITTER APPS & TOOLS

Social media can be time consuming, no matter which platform you use. You can log into Twitter or Facebook with the intention of posting a quick update to your fans, then lose yourself down a rabbit warren of links, comments strands, and articles. Many artists don't like to use social media for that reason, explaining that it takes up too much of their time, and that the hours they spend learning a new platform, or staying up to date on a current platform could be better spent creating something instead.

While I'm clearly an advocate for the benefits of social media, I understand these concerns. I'll admit that sometimes it can seem as though social media is a black hole for time and a catalyst for procrastination.

Fortunately, it doesn't have to be that way. There are plenty of tools called apps – short for applications – available that reduce the amount of time you spend on social media. They make it easier by condensing hours of actions down to quick, pre-scheduled tasks.

I'd like to start by noting the importance of making sure that any tools you use are safe and legitimate. Using them often requires signing in with your Twitter username and password. This allows the app to have access to some of your information. To ensure that you don't have your account stolen, I'd recommend only using reputable apps with millions of users. Even then, read the fine print to see what those apps can do if you give them access to your account. Making a mistake here can turn a time-saving venture into a massive setback. Don't let that stop you from experimenting, though. Some apps are a blessing to the creative professional. Depending on how many features you want access to, most Twitter apps have both free and paid versions, so you can generally trial them first.

Part of this chapter will discuss the advantages of investing in some free or cheap and very useful tools that will help you to manage a substantial Twitter following. Some of the tools and strategies can be implemented if you've only got a small number of followers, but they tend to work more effectively for influential accounts – the bigger, the better.

SCHEDULING APPS

Good scheduling apps are an essential tool in your social media inventory. Some of the most popular ones like Hootsuite and Buffer have millions of happy users who schedule posts weeks or even months in advance. Doing so means that you don't have to visit Twitter several times every day to post new content. Scheduling apps make you seem omnipresent even if you actually only log in once every few days to respond to comments.

I personally don't use scheduling apps as I like my posts to be spontaneous and live. This tactic has led me to have an interaction rate that is far higher than the industry average, possibly due to the amount of genuine interaction in my tweets. However, I wouldn't disregard scheduling apps completely. If you're an avid blogger and want to post links to content you've written then scheduling apps are a good way to do this, driving constant traffic to your website. Even without blogs, many people rely on scheduling apps to maintain their day-to-day online presence or to help them stay active when they go away.

One scheduling app that can be extremely useful is Thunderclap – an app that helps to coordinate your tweets with other users so that you can try to get something trending on Twitter. This app is useful when running advertising campaigns as it enables the organiser to get people to sign up to Thunderclap's tweet-scheduling service in which they all opt to tweet a pre-selected template message at the same time.

Using a tool like Thunderclap can be much more successful and reliable than having to count on forgetful supporters to come through for you on the day of a product launch or event. It can offer a better chance of hitting that coveted trending hashtag list next to Twitter's main feed.

For more information on this tool, see the section on Thunderclap in the chapter "Harnessing the Power of #Hashtags."

MANAGEFLITTER

This is an app that I use every day and have grown to trust so much that I decided to move from the free to the paid version a year ago as it provides extra benefits.

ManageFlitter is a popular Twitter app that has over 3 million users. Roughly 1% of Twitter's users use ManageFlitter. What it does is provide you with a breakdown of the people you follow on Twitter, separating them into categories like

"Not Following Back", "No Profile Image", "Non-English", and "Inactive", amongst others.

Within these categories, it also enables you to sort the people you follow into various orders, including by follower number, level of activity, and influence. All of this makes the pruning exercise so much easier. The basic service is totally free and there's no catch.

ManageFlitter encourages you to allow them to send automated tweets about their service with your account but you can turn off that option. That way, they won't alienate your audience with stats about your followers and growth.

You can use ManageFlitter to unfollow people on their website. It still has to be a manual process in which you unfollow each person individually as automating the unfollowing process breaches Twitter's terms and could get your account suspended. However, the way the app organises accounts streamlines the procedure considerably.

If you're going to use ManageFlitter and you're not reading this book from cover to cover then I recommend you read about my unfollowing process which focuses on maximising your chance of being followed back and not getting suspended from Twitter.

ManageFlitter has a function called "Never Unfollow." Once you click this option on an account, ManageFlitter won't include it in its lists when suggesting people to unfollow. The reason for this is so that you can't unfollow them without specifically entering a list entitled "Never Unfollow". You will still be able to unfollow them on Twitter itself but that should be less of a problem as Twitter doesn't allow for bulk unfollows in the same way that ManageFlitter does so should cause fewer mistakes.

You could test the Never Unfollow list for yourself by starting with your role models so that you never unfollow them accidentally. I personally also use the feature as damage control on the rare occasions when I unfollow someone that I think has become inactive and then they call me out on it. In this scenario, I simply apologise for the mistake, re-follow them, and then add them to my Never Unfollow list to ensure that it never happens again.

Using the Never Unfollow list should be enough to stop you from losing your priority followers – at least by unfollowing them. As for giving them priority attention, that's where the second level of security comes into action.

MANAGEFLITTER PRO

I decided to move from ManageFlitter's free package to the paid version, ManageFlitter Pro, shortly after I hit 30,000 followers. I wish I had done this sooner due to the amount of time it saves me that I can now spend on writing books.

The main difference between the two is Pro's added "Power Mode" function (found in the bottom left-hand corner of the app's panel).

Before using Pro I used to find prospective followers by scouring the follower lists of other authors, manually searching for users who match my desired criteria. Power Mode enables you to enter these criteria into a form which then filters Twitter accounts until it finds matches. As it allows you to use multiple filters at once, you can efficiently scout out the most suitable potential followers; active users who are relevant to you and likely to take an interest in your work. These are real people who tend to follow back accounts that follow them and who will engage deeply with your tweets.

After Pro has found anything between tens and thousands of accounts that match your desired criteria, you will then have the option to sort them into a variety of orders of relevance. As well as that, the app also allows you to alternate between following and unfollowing groups of accounts so that you don't create sharp spikes and troughs in your following and unfollowing patterns. Doing this avoids alerting Twitter's policing systems.

The final stage of using this service is to follow and unfollow chosen accounts. This has to be done individually by clicking a "follow" or "unfollow" button to work your way through the actions you have just requested. ManageFlitter can't automate clicks for you for free as that would breach Twitter's rules and could cause trouble for both the company and you.

As you scale up your operation and aim for an ever steeper rate of growth, you will find yourself in need of a service like ManageFlitter Pro. It certainly saved me time, cutting my workload from over three hours per day to around one hour, and less if I choose not to grow in this way every day.

Operating this process later leads to organic growth. I no longer *need* to grow manually as my account now attracts a few dozen followers daily. I know this because I've taken breaks and my account continues to gain quality followers even when I go for days without logging in. However, I continue using the manual process I've described as it helps me to grow more rapidly than by organic means alone.

Besides saving me time, ManageFlitter Pro has also fine-tuned my process ethically, ensuring that I only target relevant potential followers and only follow people that I have never followed before. Maintaining the quality of your new followers, while also increasing your rate of growth without mistakenly refollowing the same people, means that you accumulate more and more relevance in your field without risking being reported by disgruntled users. As a result, you become less at risk of suspension. The more influential you are on Twitter, the less the platform wants to lose you as your involvement becomes an attractive asset.

TWITTER APPS CHECKLIST

In summary, you should:

- o Research what sort of online tools exist and what they do.
- o Consider the benefits and drawbacks of scheduling tweets.
- o Analyse whether you really need to use any apps.
- o Look up the potential dangers of signing up to a bad app.
- o Check whether an app is safe and legitimate before giving it access to your Twitter account.
- o Use apps like Thunderclap to get other people involved in your product launches and events.
- o Use an app like Manageflitter to streamline your growth tactics.
- o Start small when using apps to ensure they don't put your account in danger of being suspended by Twitter.
- o Maintain and scale your app usage over time if you see any benefits to using them.
- O Weigh up the costs of paying for a premium app against the time it can save you in the long term.

SPEEDING UP YOUR GROWTH

Growing too slowly on Twitter can mean a delay in reaching your audience, while growing aggressively is asking to get your account suspended. As a cautious person, I started slowly. That's why it took 16 months to gain my first 10,000 followers – a feat that I have since been able to replicate in two months because I now know how to grow, what tools to use, and how far I can push Twitter.

The information in this section is tried and tested and is designed for careful, incremental growth. It can gain you thousands of followers and a lot of influence over a relatively short period of time. If you adopt a steady, systematic process you can grow your following without getting suspended.

Results can come fairly quickly, but not without some effort and planning. If you cut corners and try to game the system, you are likely to lose your account. This section will take you through the steps you need in order to grow your following safely.

ORGANIC GROWTH

This type of growth is the one Twitter recommends. It involves following a handful of people who interest you and tweeting quality content. This model works well if you're a household name as people will quickly flock to your Twitter account, growing your follower numbers and influence.

However, If you aren't a superstar or a major influencer elsewhere, then growing your Twitter account organically will be relatively slow. Organic growth works fastest for people who can bring an existing fan base from elsewhere to Twitter.

PROMOTED GROWTH

Paying Twitter to promote your account or tweets to a wider audience is another strategy. To do this you simply fill in an online form including your bank account details and a budget for your campaign. Then you wait for Twitter to place your account at the top of selected lists, and your tweets ahead of unpaid ones in feeds so that your words are exposed to as many people as possible, resulting in more followers. You don't get charged for the amount of time you get promoted, but for each time someone clicks on your advert.

I believe that better ways to grow exist for those working on a small or non-existent budget. However, if you have got an advertising budget and want to try this method, here are some guideline prices.

Using this method will cost between $0.50 and $4.00 for each advert click, with the average click costing $2.50, based on Twitter's bidding system. Prices vary as the system is based on a bidding model where those who bid the most get priority over less ambitious bidders. You can pay a lot less, but Twitter will punish that by slowing your growth.

While paying per click is measurable, clicks don't necessarily lead to new followers. For every person who clicks on an advert, only a tiny proportion of them will follow you. As a result, the cost per follower is actually much higher than the price you bid. In the event of a famous person following you as a result of the advert, it is possible, of course, that costs could be reduced considerably as that person's attention could bring with it lots of new followers who probably have not seen your promotion. You wouldn't get charged for those extra followers as they will not have found you through the ad itself.

Likewise, if you're a famous brand – for example, the publisher Penguin, who I know used this method for a short time – then this may be a more viable option as their follow back percentage would be likely to be much higher than that of an unknown artist.

For the rest of us, however, I believe this option is inefficient and too expensive to be cost effective.

CREATING A HIGH PRIORITY TRIBE

Your high priority tribe contains your most attentive followers. They are often people who you will never have encountered before joining Twitter.

You will have built up good relationships with them over time and will know something about their lives, as they will yours. They will send you tweets about things they're doing on a regular basis, as well as taking an interest in your activities. These are people who, over time, might drop out of your ideal follower guidelines in terms of having poor follow ratios and imperfect activity levels, but when it comes to you, they do interact. As a result, you need to take great care not to unfollow them.

As you grow and begin to unfollow accounts in greater numbers, accidentally unfollowing members of your high priority tribe can become a problem. Genuine followers can sometimes slip through the net and find themselves being unfollowed by you on your quest for expansion. Fortunately, I've devised a double-layer security plan to stop this from happening so you never unfollow your best supporters.

The first layer involves putting your most engaged followers into lists. Being selective when entering certain followers into lists means that you can dip in every once in a while and ensure that you haven't unfollowed them accidentally without the task taking up too much time. The other security layer I've devised only applies to those using the premium version of the Twitter app ManageFlitter, but it's the most effective in my experience. All you have to do is simply hand pick some of your favourite followers and put them into a "Never Unfollow" group. For more information on these methods, look at the section on ManageFlitter in "Twitter Apps and Tools."

"SUGGESTED BY TWITTER" GROWTH

For most people, this train has already left the station. When you create an account, Twitter will suggest a handful of people to follow that they think might be of interest to you. These are accounts "suggested by Twitter." They are often established, influential figures that have gained massive levels of engagement and are being suggested to you based on preferences and interests that you have expressed. For example, if you click "Music" then Twitter will suggest pop stars and musicians.

It's still possible to get into the elite group of accounts Twitter chooses to promote if you post regularly and have plenty of content that you're constantly promoting. However, this position is almost exclusively reserved for early adopters –

those who took advantage of Twitter's limited choice during its infancy – and A-listers who have accumulated sudden, global success.

On her influential blog, publishing expert Jane Friedman talks about how she was put on this list as a possible point of interest for writers and publishing professionals. As a result, her account saw rapid and sustained growth. She now has over 215,000 followers and admits that her phenomenal success is partly due to Twitter rewarding her for being an early adopter. The company put her ahead of other equally capable people by suggesting her account as a point of interest for new users who expressed an interest in writing.

It's still possible to gain a coveted place as one of Twitter's suggested accounts, but you can't control the process.

UNFOLLOWING FOR GROWTH

One problem you will very quickly come up against is reaching the limit on the amount of people you can follow. In order to break through this ceiling you'll need to unfollow people that aren't interested in what you have to say.

Initially this means unfollowing accounts that don't follow you back. Now I'm not saying you have to apply this rule to everyone. In fact, I follow a number of people that will probably never follow me back. I do this because they interest me and I like to see what they have to say. I would encourage you to do this, too. After all, enjoying Twitter will help you stick at it long enough to see the long-term benefits.

Apart from this select group of users, I have to prune the number of people I follow regularly in order to grow at a steady rate. Twitter stops its users from following more than 5,000 people unless they have at least 4,545 followers themselves. Only when you've passed that threshold can you follow more people. However, passing that glass ceiling doesn't mean you can follow as many people as you want. Even then, it limits you to being able to follow 10% more people than your own follower count.

You can exceed this barrier by maintaining a good following-to-follower ratio. As a business, getting this balance right doesn't matter so much. People expect companies to follow lots of people as they follow potential customers. Businesses only have to keep their ratio relatively even so that they can keep growing.

However, as an individual you're expected to get a good ratio to show that you're someone worth following. It also provides a form of social proof, persuading people that they should follow you because they're missing out on something if they don't. Having a good ratio makes you look less like a business and more like a stellar personality that people *want* to follow. There are reasons, of course, why you shouldn't prune the number of people you follow down to a handful when you have thousands of followers.

For a start, some potentially good contacts won't follow you if they think you won't reciprocate their follow. Plus, unfollowing everyone will mean insulting some of your most active followers and losing their loyalty. Focus on unfollowing people effectively without damaging your Twitter account's growing influence.

Unfollowing can be problematic and time consuming if you do it manually on Twitter. This is why most people who chose to use the same growth method as me tend to use Twitter apps to help streamline the process. There are several reliable apps that can help you but I would be careful when choosing one as they all have different terms and conditions. It's paramount that you read what information and abilities you're handing to them before you accept their terms.

GROWING A DELAYED UNFOLLOW LIST

As a new account, you should follow several accounts each day and wait for a proportion of them to follow back. After a week you can start unfollowing. Leaving it seven days before beginning to unfollow accounts means that you will build what I call a "delayed unfollow list" – a list of accounts that you will unfollow sequentially in the chronological order that you followed them if they haven't followed you back within a few days. As long as you only unfollow a small portion of the number of people you follow every day, you will always stay a week behind your delayed unfollow list. There are several reasons why you need to do this.

A delayed unfollow list gives the people you follow a few days to get online and follow you back. If they don't do it in that time, then the chances are that they either aren't interested in following you or they don't go on Twitter often enough to see that you've followed them and so are unlikely to interact much even if they did follow you back. This practice also lowers the risk of your account getting suspended. Accounts that regularly follow lots of users and then unfollow them within a day or two may be seen as spammers and get suspended. By waiting a week to unfollow, you avoid this rapid churning behaviour and keep your account safe from Twitter's policing algorithms.

Make sure that your delayed unfollow list doesn't get too long or too short. This requires you to unfollow a varying number of people, depending on what is necessary to maintain that balance. It may seem like an extra inconvenience to think about but maintaining a delayed unfollow list is crucial if you want to grow safely.

SAVING TIME AS YOU EXPAND

After you've mastered the art of who to follow, how many people to follow, the best type of content to post, and when it's safe to unfollow people who don't follow you back, the next step to achieving a thriving Twitter following is scaling up and getting a good following-to-follower ratio.

To scale up, all you have to do is incrementally expand the numbers as your follower count grows. The process doesn't get more complicated, it only gets more time-consuming. At least, it does when you use the free version of ManageFlitter.

When I started growing my Twitter following, my daily process took about half an hour. As my account grew and I followed more people during each session and replied to more tweets, this process expanded to fill an hour, then two hours, then three. This doesn't have to be the case, so if you don't think you have enough time for that sort of commitment then don't worry. I made the decision to grow at an exponential rate but you don't have to do that. Work at the speed that's comfortable for you. You'll still grow. Your growth might just be a little slower. I enjoy this process and love Twitter. For me, it's an integral part of my job as an author. Others may want to focus on promoting their work differently and only spend a portion of their free time on social media.

I decided to switch to the paid version of ManageFlitter (Manageflitter Pro) when I reached 30,000 followers, simply because Twitter was taking up over three hours of my time every day.

When I started paying for the service (which is only $12 dollars per month at the time I'm writing this) I tripled the amount of work I did in one session and it took me only a third of the time! Now I only spend about an hour working on Twitter every day, and that's only because I'm constantly looking for better ways to grow and reach new readers. In hindsight, I wish I'd made the switch at about 10,000 followers. If you're serious about rapidly growing your audience, I'd advise that you use productivity tools to make the process easier and faster.

For smaller accounts with fewer than 10,000 followers, ManageFlitter Pro would be overkill. Focus on growing a small, loyal follower base at first and gain a reputation for delivering quality content before you expand on a massive scale.

SPEEDING UP YOUR GROWTH CHECKLIST

So, to summarise, you should:

o Tweet quality content to maximise your organic growth.

o Consider whether paying Twitter to promote your account is the best strategy for you.

o Build a high priority tribe based on your most loyal followers.

o Keep your high priority followers engaged.

o Follow lots of relevant accounts to grow rapidly.

o Identify people who are uninterested in your account.

o Unfollow those people so you never hit Twitter's glass ceiling.

o Keep a check on Twitter's limits to keep your account safe.

o Exploit as much of Twitter's limits as possible to ensure fast growth.

o Make sure your follower growth is targeted and ethical to maintain a high level of interactions.

o Form a delayed unfollow list to protect your account from being suspended.

o Scale up your activities to grow faster.

o Consider using tools to save you time as you expand.

o Achieve a good ratio to offer social proof to prospective followers.

MEASURING YOUR INFLUENCE

There are better ways to measure your growth on Twitter than counting your followers from one day to the next. A more useful measurement is the engagement your tweets get on a regular basis. You will always post anomalous tweets that get far more, or far fewer, interactions than your others but there should typically be an upward trend in the level of interactions they achieve over time.

Starting on Twitter can often mean going days without having any interactions. Don't let this dishearten you. I aim to get at least one good interaction (a retweet, like, or comment) for every 3,000 followers – which is better than most celebrities, despite sounding meagre. If you only have 50 followers then many of your tweets won't get any engagement at all – and that's not necessarily your fault. Many of your international followers could be asleep when you tweet. Lots could be offline. That doesn't matter. You'll gain traction eventually.

Generally, I first saw a jump in my level of retweets, likes, and comments when my account passed 3,000 followers. Then I saw a larger jump at 10,000, but that was nothing compared to the tsunami of interactions that started happening when I hit the 50,000 follower milestone. Nowadays, I average around

20 replies, 45 retweets, and 185 likes every day. And those numbers keep increasing. I still have slumps in engagement, usually between 8am and noon UK time when many of my American followers are asleep, but I've found that I can tweet at pretty much any time now and get some responses.

KLOUT SCORE

Klout is an independent company that tracks all of the interactions you get on Facebook, Twitter, LinkedIn, Instagram, and other social media sites, then converts them into a score between one and 100. The higher your Klout score, the greater your internet influence is.

Each consecutive number is more difficult to get than the previous one, so progression requires a more impressive show of influence than you've managed before. Your Klout score is measured by the number of interactions your content receives. However, certain types of interactions are given more weight in this calculation than others. Like Twitter, Klout doesn't release details of its algorithms. However, what is apparent is that Klout favours retweets over likes on Twitter.

What interests me about Klout is that it promotes the importance of interactions over follower numbers. For this reason, Barack Obama currently has the world's highest Klout score, despite having fewer Twitter followers than pop stars with more followers. Everyone's score changes daily. If you don't maintain your social media delivery then you will see your Klout score drop after just 24 hours. It reflects public opinion and warns you on a daily basis if you're becoming more or less relevant.

Although its relevance has been questioned, Klout is taken very seriously by those working in the creative industries. In the US, many advertising companies take into account a person's Klout score when considering whether or not to hire them. The average score is 40 and many companies encourage their staff to maintain a score above 50. Their logic is that if you can't promote yourself effectively then you probably can't promote their business. This is less evident outside the US, but it still exists.

"But I'm not an advertising exec," I hear you say. Well that doesn't matter. If you're a creative professional then contacts will want to know that you have a supportive audience on social media. If you don't then you could miss out on lucrative promotional opportunities like speaking engagements that might otherwise be given to people with a higher Klout score.

It doesn't just stop with jobs. Again this is mostly relevant in the US, but your Twitter presence could also benefit your personal life. Many businesses prioritise influential customers. It's been documented that certain hotels discretely look up their guests' Klout score and then offer better service, possibly in the form of free drinks or a room upgrade, to their most influential visitors. The assumption is that guests with higher Klout scores are more able to spread praise or damaging remarks than less influential clients. The same goes for airlines. If there are two passengers who have problems with their seats, the one with the higher Klout score may be more likely to get an upgrade because of their influence.

I once accidently left a coat on an aeroplane then later reported it missing. When I returned to the airport to leave the country, I remember an extremely determined employee running, red-faced, after my plane's shuttle-bus with my coat. On handing it to me, she whispered, "If you'd like to mention

our good service on social media, we'd really appreciate it."
Then she pressed a card with the airport's Twitter and
Facebook details into my palm. This may just be a coincidence,
but I couldn't help but wonder if all of that effort was due to
me having 60,000 Twitter followers and a Klout score of 61 at
the time.

Keep on top of your Klout score. It's a great indication of
your authority and could offer some real-life benefits that you
might not expect. You may never realise that you're being
prioritised for this reason, but it will be working in your favour,
motivating strangers around you to go to great lengths to keep
you happy.

Twitter Analytics

This term may sound like jargon but if you want to measure
your social media growth then there isn't really a better way to
do it than looking at your analytics. You can find the analytics
page in the dropdown menu at the top right-hand corner of
your profile.

Clicking on it will reveal pages of information that are
massively useful if you want to learn how best to optimise your
tweets.

Twitter Analytics can show you information regarding your
followers' activities, their nationalities, their economic status,
their interests, your top new followers, your most engaged

tweets, and a wealth of other information that can help you deliver the best possible content to your audience.

QUALITATIVE GROWTH

Other than using numerical stats, you could judge your growth on the increasing quality of interactions you receive. All of these little moments show you just how much your Twitter followers are enriching your life as your influence grows. This type of growth isn't something that can always be measured.

It is possible for your Twitter following to shrink in number. The number of interactions your tweets get could also decrease. However, even if you lose followers from a quantitative perspective, you may still benefit from the quality of followers you've gained. Remember: the quality of your supporters should always be given more significance than the quantity.

MEASURING YOUR INFLUENCE CHECKLIST

To see benefits from measuring your influence, you should:

o   Recognise the need to grow your influence as a creative professionals.
o   Decide the best ways to measure your success.
o   Aim to improve your Klout score.
o   Break down all the information Twitter Analytics provides to maximise the impact of your tweets.
o   Consider the qualitative growth you've experienced as well as quantitative growth when making strategic decisions.

REACHING BEYOND TWITTER

Twitter probably isn't going to be around forever. As with any social media platform, it will eventually fall out of fashion. There's one exception to this rule – that being Facebook – but without diversifying and evolving, even that would have fallen away years ago. Remember how everyone was once on Bebo, MySpace, and Windows Live Messenger? If you don't, then that just reinforces my point. Those social networks were huge. They seemed too powerful to fail. And yet, where are they now? They still exist but now have a much-reduced user base.

So, what's the point of investing time and effort into any social media platform if it's destined to fail? Well, the quick answer is opportunity. Not every platform is set up to allow you to grow a following internationally. Twitter, however, allows you to do just that – offering rapid growth and no barriers to entry. And that means there's an opportunity. It's a big break, the success of which depends almost entirely on skill rather than luck.

The key to surviving after you have been given that big break isn't just pumping out quality content and hoping that your original platform stays alive forever. That's putting all of your eggs in one basket, which is fine if you know that the basket is indestructible, but not if there's even a slight chance of it breaking your eggs. What I suggest is that you should also begin to look for other ways to diversify your brand. That way, even if Twitter fails, you and your work will survive.

PERISCOPE

The simplest, but riskiest, way to diversify is to spread yourself across several branches of the same platform. It's risky because all of those platforms are owned by the same company. But it's simpler than starting again on an unrelated platform because your existing audience is more likely to follow you.

Think of it like this; if you have a healthy following on Google+ and want to spread your brand in case Google+ collapsed, the easiest place to start would be on YouTube. As YouTube is owned by Google and is integrated with Google+, growing a YouTube audience would be simple because many of your followers are likely to use both. The fact that they are both owned by the same company means that instability remains. If Google finds its market share declining quickly then it could shut down both Google+ and YouTube to focus on other projects, destroying your entire following and leaving you to build your audience from scratch.

If you want to start small on your diversification, you may want to try Periscope, a new addition to Twitter that shares videos filmed directly from mobile phones. Content there only lasts a few hours before disappearing forever. It's a great new way to present your personality to your Twitter audience because it shows them that you're a real person. Video makes you a figure in someone's life; a friend, not just a message on a screen.

Delivering video content is a very different skill to

tweeting. If you're naturally funny or have something fascinating to say then it's a viable option. Stars of social media sites like Vine and YouTube got huge followings not just because they had original ideas but because they were likable and used that likability to grow massive, loyal audiences. Others who were every bit as original, but not quite so charismatic, have perished.

I've personally considered using video but question whether it's the right platform for me because the written word is my strongest mode of communication. Plus, I recognise that it's a massive undertaking. Before beginning your voyage into online video, first consider whether or not you have the time and talent to make such a commitment. In the world of video content, consistency and on-screen likeability are the fastest ways to get to the top.

Another thing to think about if you're planning to use Periscope is that an audience isn't built overnight. Your existing Twitter audience will help to push you off the bottom, but only some of them will make the transition. You will still need to master the new site with its strange rules to build a powerful audience there. This means being prolific and consistent.

YouTubers profess the need to be able to release relevant videos on regular days like a TV show. Lacking consistency with these deadlines can result in a disappointed audience who feel that you have been unprofessional. If you feel that you have sufficient content, and that you can deliver consistently, then this is definitely the platform for you.

DRIVING TRAFFIC *EN MASSE*

When I first discovered that growing a trusted relationship with my Twitter followers meant being able to drive lots of traffic to other social networks, blogs, and sales pages, it was a eureka moment.

It can help you diversify your brand beyond Twitter. Plus there are many other benefits. I've monitored this by including links in my tweets, then using the handy stats button, which looks like a bar chart and can be found underneath any tweet, to measure the number of link clicks these efforts have spawned.

Tweet Activity		
	Impressions	22,763
Daniel Parsons @dkparsonswriter		
It's taken 7 months but I finally have a cool, new author website that gives out free ebooks!	Total engagements	493
http://danielparsonsbooks.com/ Check it out, guys!	Link clicks	197
	Likes	145
Reach a bigger audience	Retweets	65
Get more engagements by promoting this Tweet		

What I found is that I can direct followers to any web page I recommend with a single tweet. One destination I tried is my blog that, despite only having a few posts that talk about publishing as an indie author, now attracts hundreds of hits every day. This success possibly happened because, over a long period of time, I've accumulated a strong following of other indie authors at various stages in their career. Prospective writers who are new to the business, and some established authors who are always looking for new ideas, have followed links to articles I've written, and posted comments on my blog as a result of a tweet. This, in turn, has helped my website to climb the Google search results ladder and has led to new readers stumbling upon my work.

A blog is a great way to begin what is called "content marketing" – sharing knowledge that other people want in exchange for their continued support. This often comes in the form of a mailing list signup, or book sales.

Some of the people I follow avidly started their relationship with me in a similar way, drawing me in with worthwhile blog posts that led me to recognise them as experts.

If you want to go down this route, then a blog that is supported by your Twitter account is a great way to offer your author platform more stability. If you host the blog yourself and purchase the domain name then nobody can pull that platform out from under you. Plus, you can generate extra income from your blog by recommending products and gaining commission from them by using affiliate links. This works especially well if they are products that you know your audience will definitely need and/or want.

Another way I've used Twitter to help me to diversify was to venture into the global, story-sharing website called Wattpad.

Now I admit that the examples in this part of the book will exclusively apply to writers, but if you're a musician you can pretty much replace "Wattpad" with "YouTube" and get similar results. On Wattpad, authors, poets, journalists, and other types of writers can post content of any length for public viewing. Wattpad users can then read that content for free. This sounds like a terrible business model if you're a writer as you don't make any money from it. However, this process *can* be monetised.

Wattpad's algorithms favour longer content like novels. Chapters will often be posted episodically over a few weeks or months. If you have good reach on Twitter then you have weeks to advertise that story to all of those people in the same way a TV show builds over time. You're driving traffic to great, free content, not requesting sales through advertising. As a result, you keep your reputation as someone who isn't a spammer, and your work gains valuable exposure.

Using Twitter to garner extra attention on Wattpad helped me to grow an audience there with relative ease. The extra traffic won my work a place on Wattpad's featured page, which got my work read thousands of times over the following months.

This tactic isn't exclusive to Wattpad. When it comes to promoting on Twitter, the same method can be used to grow an audience on YouTube, Vine, or Tumblr. It's all about growing your audience steadily and allowing small successes in the early stages to help you aim for bigger successes later.

The momentum this method generated actually built a completely new Wattpad audience made up of readers who were attracted to my work because of the attention it was getting from my Twitter followers. Suddenly, people started asking when I was releasing new chapters. They knew me for my work, not just my tweets. I switched from being a Twitter user who wrote to being a writer who uses Twitter. There was an overnight shift, and because of my reach on Twitter, my readers got to connect with each other via the comments under my tweets.

Then, Wattpad took notice of the attention my work was getting and featured the 37-page horror story on their horror page. Soon after, it reached number 37 in the Wattpad horror chart and amassed around 30,000 reads, as well as being added to a list entitled "Top Zombie Stories" which the site used as part of a marketing campaign for a major Hollywood zombie movie.

Of course, driving traffic from Twitter to another free

platform doesn't necessarily make you money. However, monetising this free process is actually pretty simple. All you have to do is release your whole work – in this case a full story – on Kindle or another similar paid platform before you upload your first chapter to Wattpad. Then, at the end of each chapter, you say that the full version of the story is available on these platforms and tell your readers that they can purchase the whole thing to read if they can't wait for the next chapter to be made available for free. The same method can be applied to songs released on YouTube by musicians as parts of an album, or game levels released as a free version of an app by a video game developer.

Many people won't buy something if they can get it for free online. However, they will pay extra if they can experience that content in the way that they want, and when they want it.

You might be tempted to roll out a series of chapters, each ending with the promotional message I mentioned above, and then never release the end of the story for free. Surely, that would mean hooking readers and then keeping your window of opportunity open forever, right? Well, not exactly. There are several reasons why you shouldn't do this. One is that you owe it to your audience to keep your promise and give them closure on the story. If they are willing to take a chance on trying your work, then the least you can do is give them a satisfying ending. If you are confident in the ending then you shouldn't have a problem with giving it away. If people know that you create great endings that still leave them wanting more then this will actually work in your favour when it comes to getting readers moving on to paying for the rest of your work.

I've experienced this phenomenon first-hand. As a result of readers sampling my work on Wattpad, several have tweeted to let me know that they went on to purchase my other books on Amazon. Some bought my entire back catalogue and left glowing reviews. When you think about it, it makes perfect business sense to use this try-before-you-buy strategy. That's why I'm still giving away that 37-page story for free to this day, and why I will give away more stories in the future.

REAL-WORLD LEVERAGE

The benefits of Twitter don't stop in the virtual world, either. Having a strong following can provide useful leverage in the real world. Even if you aren't monetising your Twitter following yet, lots of people are impressed by large numbers. If you say you have 20,000 followers, get mentioned 200 times every month by strangers on Twitter, and your tweets reach around 100,000 people every 30 days then people take notice. Don't be self-deprecating of your achievements if people try to praise you. Being humble makes you likable but putting yourself down can cause you to miss out on opportunities. If people want to praise you for your achievements, let them.

For me, this came in the form of courses. As a young author who doesn't come from a well-connected family, I knew I had to get my voice heard some other way. I needed a method that was cheap and scalable over time so I could grow. That way was Twitter. When I talked to the other authors in my local area about my success, they wanted to know how I managed it. Knowing that I couldn't fit a comprehensive answer into a quick conversation, I started running Twitter seminars for creative professionals.

While on stage at a book festival, someone in the room asked how many followers I had on Twitter and that's when I first noticed the power of the numbers. Now, as you know, I value engagement levels over numbers of followers but, in cases like this, numbers hook an audience. My answer – then around 50,000 followers – caused an audible gasp that rippled through the room. Suddenly people took me seriously. Several authors approached me after the announcement to network with me. Twitter can open doors for you as a creative professional that you might struggle to open without it.

Using the power of numbers has also allowed me access to celebrity authors. I once asked a bestselling author I met at a bookshop if he would like to be interviewed for my blog. After a moment of hesitation on his part, I told him my plans to promote the interview to my thousands of Twitter followers. After that, he gladly agreed to it because it offered him a platform to promote his own work. Of course, I didn't mind his intentions. In the creative arts, collaboration is more effective than competition and his big name would attract more readers to my website. It was a win-win situation.

Aside from these two notable moments, I've also judged a creative writing competition and sat on an author panel at a literary event purely due to my influence on Twitter.

These are just some of the ways that your Twitter followers can help you to expand your influence beyond Twitter itself. Twitter opened avenues that I never knew existed beforehand – and there's still so much more potential to explore.

As social media evolves, so must we. Gone are the times when producing remarkable work guaranteed you success. Of course, that's still important, but it's often not enough to ensure success on its own.

REACHING BEYOND TWITTER CHECKLIST

To extend your influence beyond Twitter, you need to:

o   Understand the benefits of diversifying your brand.

o   Choose whether you want your next platform to be inside or outside Twitter's corporate umbrella.

o   Understand the challenges and rewards of establishing a presence on social media platforms outside the same corporate umbrella.

o   Test Twitter's power to drive traffic *en masse*.

O   Use your online influence as leverage in real-world situations.

A FINAL NOTE

Establishing a powerful voice on Twitter and using that voice to build a trustworthy brand is achievable. All it requires is a basic understanding of Twitter's culture, a simple grasp of social media algorithms, and creativity to keep improving the quality and quantity of your interactions. Embracing this will take you and your brand from strength to strength.

Getting to the level and quality of exposure that I currently enjoy on Twitter has taken me almost four years. Fortunately, this guide will fast-track your results, guiding you around some of the pitfalls that slowed my progress. As a result, you can focus your energy into those critical hours needed to create the all-important art upon which your dream career is founded.

Good luck! I guess I'll be seeing you on Twitter. Oh, before you go, I have one more thing to discuss with you...

WHAT TO DO NEXT

I hope that, if nothing else, this book has taught you just how much I value my followers and readers. Their help and generosity is what has made this book possible. With that in mind, I'd like to explain a couple of small things you could do that would make a massive difference to the success of this project.

PLEASE REVIEW THIS BOOK ON AMAZON

Firstly, the most helpful thing you could do is review this book on Amazon, Goodreads, and any other reading platforms you use. Many readers don't realise the power of good reviews. The more, the better! Having a few extra four or five star reviews can give an author a competitive edge when applying for advertising from advertising companies whose mailing lists can lead to life-changing success. I'd really appreciate it!

RECOMMEND THE #ARTOFTWITTER ON TWITTER

I'd love to hear your thoughts on Twitter. If you still have questions after reading this book then you can contact me on Twitter via my handle @dkparsonswriter or give me suggestions on things you would like me to include in a future edition or another book.

If you want to discuss something with me that can't be condensed into 140 characters then you can email me via the "contact" panel on www.danielparsonsbooks.com. I aim to reply to all messages within a few days.

JOIN MY MAILING LIST

If you'd like to get updates on my latest book releases, as well as limited-time discounts and giveaways, sign up to my mailing list by following the links on www.danielparsonsbooks.com.

BE A SUCCESS STORY

The final way you could help is by becoming a success story on

Twitter and helping to make it the best social network in the world. Please try new things, work hard to grow, and do get in touch. Your success on Twitter after reading this book will be a massive indicator of whether or not I have done my job. You could even be quoted in a future edition. Good luck. Happy tweeting!

ABOUT DANIEL

Daniel Parsons lives in South Wales, UK. As well as writing *The #ArtOfTwitter*, he is the author of three fiction books for children and teenagers.

He wrote the first version of his debut book *The Winter Freak Show* while at Cardiff University studying English Literature, but has recently re-mastered and re-launched it in print. The encouraging reception it got from fellow students and other readers spurred him on to write *Blott*, a full-length teen fantasy novel, which also proved to be popular.

Daniel has also published a comedy zombie story entitled *Necroville* after it received acclaim on the story-sharing website Wattpad. There it got nearly 30,000 reads and was named one of the site's Top Zombie Stories as part of a campaign to promote the Hollywood movie *Pride and Prejudice and Zombies*.

If you want to join his 90,000+ followers on Twitter (@DKParsonsWriter), he would love to hear from you.

You can check out more info about him and his work at www.DanielParsonsBooks.com.

FICTION

BY

DANIEL PARSONS

THE WINTER FREAK SHOW

After twelve-year-old Toby Carter escapes a brutal workhouse at Christmas, he can't believe his good fortune. Adopted by a band of travelling performers called The Winter Freak Show who put on spellbinding shows each night, he finally believes he's found the family he always wanted. Then everything falls apart.

Children are disappearing throughout the city. Pretty soon, all evidence points to those Toby trusted the most and he finds himself caught up in a conspiracy far more sinister than he ever imagined. Defenceless and on the run, he's confronted with two options: uncover the kidnapper before another child falls victim or stand by and watch as the shadowy criminal becomes unstoppable.

The fate of Christmas rests in the balance.

FACE OF A TRAITOR

It's been a year since thirteen-year-old Toby Thornton found his long-lost family. But already cracks are appearing in his dream life. Forbidden from seeing his magical friends at The Winter Freak Show, he begins to realise how much he misses adventure. So when he gets word that the elves are in danger, that's all the excuse he needs to run away from home.

It isn't long before he discovers that things are worse than he imagined. Nicko has been kidnapped. And without the ringmaster's guidance, his elves have descended into chaos. A band of shapeshifting enemies lurk among their ranks. Monsters are on the loose. And the secretive mastermind behind it all is trying to resurrect the most frightening evil the elves have ever faced. Only Toby stands in their way.

If he fails, forget Christmas. This time, the human race will fall.

BLOTT

Thirteen-year-old Blott Meritum has hidden his freakish ability since he was a toddler. However, as his people hurtle toward starvation, he has no option but to risk exposure and take action.

He commits a forbidden crime to save his people, and soon discovers that the world outside the village harbours unexpected perils, and that his ability means he can change his people's whole existence. However, a sinister voice inside his head has other ideas.

Will he keep his humanity and save his people? Or will he be consumed by the monster inside him?

THE DEAD WOODS

Graduating university is an emotional time for everyone. When a group of ex-students decide to spend one last night together at a zombie experience facility to create lasting memories, however, none of them anticipate just how memorable it will turn out to be. It quickly becomes apparent that the undead actors are very good at what they do. Too good.

Armed with only an arsenal of Nerf guns, the group quickly figure out that they'll need more than foam bullets and sandwiches to get them through the night.

LAST CRAWL

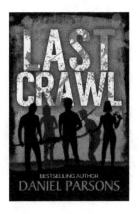

Milo's fear of everything has held him back for as long as he can remember. He knows university will drag him out of his comfort zone but he has no idea just how uncomfortable he is about to become. When zombies strike during his first night out on campus, he quickly discovers that making friends is a matter of life and death.

A chance encounter reveals that zombies don't attack extremely drunk people. Can Milo and his new flatmates band together to survive the most dangerous bar crawl the world has ever seen?

www.ingramcontent.com/pod-product-compliance
Lightning Source LLC
LaVergne TN
LVHW022342060326
832902LV00022B/4192